Adam

To Your BIG
Life!

Rom 12:2

" . . . *at last the* ladder,

which had been built
s l o w l y ,
s l o w l y ,
one hope at a time,
reached up to

the clouds.

And the dreamer *began*

to climb."

Becoming UNcommon!

Becoming UNcommon!

DEVELOPING YOUR SUCCESS AT THE SPEED OF LIFE

Michael York
Student and CEO

In celebration of the power of learning.

"To STRIVE To SEEK, To FIND, and NOT to Yield."

—Tennyson

BROWN BOOKS PUBLISHING GROUP
DALLAS, TEXAS

For information please contact
Brown Books Publishing Group
16200 North Dallas Parkway, Suite 170, Dallas, TX 75248
972-381-0009   www.brownbooks.com

First Printing 2003

ISBN 0-9726140-0-1
LCCN 2002096233

DEDICATION

"To All My Teachers
Who Have Made Me Today
A Better Student

And To My Fellow Students
Who Make Me Today
A Better Teacher"

BECOMING UNCOMMON . . .
Developing Your Success at the Speed of Life

"When Michael York shows up,
somebody's gonna learn something . . . It is amazing how
he makes people *think differently*
about something they've been doing . . .
and see things from a new perspective."

—a student

SPECIAL THANKS TO

Zig Ziglar, Jim Rohn, Charlie "*Tremendous*" Jones,
John Maxwell, Tom Peters, Ty Boyd, and
Jeffrey Gitomer
(and so many others)

Your instruction and inspiration has shaped many lives
and changed many minds, including my own. Thanks for doing
what you do, and for your contributions to my success and the
writing of this book.

And to Tony Morris, wherever you are.

To MGC,
I couldn't have done it without you!

To my mother, June Jeanette, *thank you for
your encouragement and for helping a young boy
believe he could be anything he wanted to be.*

To "The Woman."

And to my family for the fullness of my life.

You can't change people.
But if you can change the
way they think,
change their minds,
**then people will change
themselves.**
—Michael York

(to my six-year-old . . .)
"Hey son,
What did you learn today?"

(one day my six-year-old says to me)
"Hey Dad...
What did you learn today?"

WHEN WILL YOU STOP LEARNING?

Most individuals and organizations often don't **understand** the
huge difference between learning and training.
Most every company talks of the importance of training,
even providing some form of it to their workers.

But it's the attention and desire of the individual who truly
wants to learn
that is of the utmost importance.
It is this personal desire and effort to keep up, to
continue the process, that promotes real improvement.
And that is more than just training . . . it's learning.
Training has a beginning and an end,
it's for a day, or a weekend, or a convention.
And unless those attending
want to learn something, the training is for naught.

But **learning is a continuing process.** Think for a
moment about **how a six-year-old learns.**
Every day it's something new.
You might think "Hey, I'm the Daddy, I already know
it all . . ." or "I've got 15 years' experience . . ."

**The truth is, the marketplace is moving fast
beneath your feet, constantly changing.**

If you don't keep pace, or at least attempt to continue your
learning . . . **you're history.**
And this is *The Future!*

Are you excited about what you do?

About your life or your work?

How do you answer when someone asks,
"How's business," or *"How's Life treating you?"*

You know all the common answers, but how do you find
the uncommon ones?

Is there anything about your life
or your work or your legacy
you'd like to change?

It's available.

Are you?

What do you want to be known for?
How can you create positive change,
personally or professionally?

How can you learn to cultivate opportunity
from the challenges you're faced with today?

How can you get greater enjoyment
from your life?

How curious are you about the kind of success you would
love to achieve?

Don't settle.
Explore.
Don't quit.
Yet.

Finding the right answers for you and your life
isn't impossible.

It's just uncommon.

WELCOME.
This book is personal.

In it I have shared some of my most private thoughts, feelings and writings about my life, my family, and my work.

It is intended only as a means of expressing to you
Encouragement,
Instruction,
Inspiration,
and Confirmation.

That *your life* can be one of the next Great Success Stories.
My hope for you is that you will one day
share your experiences with another student.

What you choose to do for a living is your profession, but it will make up a large part of, and have an impact on, your personal life and the lives of those around you. That alone should cause you to look at your work, your contribution, your success, in new ways.

My favorite definition of success?

It's at the end of this book.
And the best part about reading this book is that you can go there now, or open it to any page between here and there and begin reading.

Be as adventurous as you like.
There are no chapters and the text flow is certainly *uncommon*.

I do not ask that you agree with everything written here, only that you consider it as you would anything personal shared with you

by a friend.

BEFORE YOU READ THIS BOOK . . .

Many of the references throughout this book are regarding sales, selling, and sales people. The reason?

Simple enough.
This book is written from a sales perspective on business and life.
Whether you realize it or not, you will "sell" your entire life.

You will . . .
Sell yourself to adults as a child.
Sell yourself to your teachers and friends in school.
Sell your attitude and your character to win your first job.
And one day,
sell your future spouse on spending a lifetime with you.
Soon after, your children will begin
selling you.

Your education throughout the various "selling" stages in life is largely up to you. Oh, there are lots of teachers and instruction available.
But rarely will those teachers come and take you captive.
You will learn these lessons primarily because you decide to.
If you have the desire to learn, or if you develop it.
So whether or not you consider yourself a "sales" person matters little.

There are principles and ideas and fundamentals
within these pages that apply to
your life and how you live it, balancing all
the pressures and demands of life's arena today.

There are lots of books and lists and tapes and videos. So it's not that we need more "how to."

It's more about you really having the "want to" or the desire and choosing to find the clues of success. They're out there.

Good hunting. And good selling.

I wish you well in your pursuit of the uncommon lessons of success in life.

Thank you for being my customer, and for being a student.

BECOMING A STUDENT
I'm Michael York, and I am a student.

→

I know that because it says so on my business card.
Actually I put it there to remind me every time
I see it, or each time someone comments on it, that it is my
goal to ALWAYS continue learning.

With all that I have learned over the past 20 years, I can now
be called a professional. There's an interesting word,
professional. Stop for a moment and think about what it means.
Being a professional at anything,
means you're doing it *for a fee.*
For profit. And by definition, you strive to be at the top
of your game, whatever it is you aspire to be a professional at.

I'll never forget soon after I started my speaking and consulting
business, being introduced as a "professional speaker." Wow!
Exciting. And challenging.
Recalling that introduction on that day challenges me every day
to be the best I can be at my chosen profession.
And by doing that, the marketplace will reward me with
a greater measure of compensation.

What's your profession?
Or what do you aspire to do at a professional level?
I'm very excited to share with you some of the things I've learned
in my study and pursuit of Success . . .
and the clues that success leaves behind.

The laws, principles, rules, suggestions, fundamentals, and
philosophies that have propelled others to
amazing successes, incredible achievements, and
breakthrough accomplishments.

Much of it I found in books and tapes,
and just by paying attention. Then I applied it to my
life and career. The instruction and inspiration that has
worked for others can impact our lives in much the same way.
Beware of anyone who knows it all and tells you so.
The best teachers remain lifelong students.
The thing we know best is the existence of
those things we have not yet learned.
I have found that there is a difference
between a manager and a leader.
Between work and a job.
Between just showing up and getting the most out of every day.
A difference between the status quo and the
value that comes with life change.

I call it "becoming uncommon!"

It's not about taking shortcuts or skipping steps, it's about
rock-solid foundational principles that can absolutely make you a
better student, better leader, better father, mother, spouse, worker,
better at whatever it is you do. Or whatever you choose to do.

This book doesn't have all the answers.

In fact, it is designed primarily to promote more questions.
Questions you will ask yourself. What I have to say is really not
all that important. But what I'm asking you to consider is that
How you respond, what you think, and how you feel
about what you read here is extremely important.
Ask yourself,
"What Am I Becoming?" as a result of what you're
learning . . . or not learning. What we'll discuss in these pages
and what I hope you'll consider is, "*What am I becoming with*
what I'm doing in life?"
I want to challenge you to take a hard look at
what you're doing . . . or not doing.

Ask yourself, "Am I *excited about what* I *do?*"

Are you? Do you love what you do? If not, what would you change? What would you love to do if you could? *Why can't you? Why don't you?*

What could make you more passionate?

Give you a zest, a zeal, a love for your work? Is there a fire burning in you? Are you excited and enthusiastic? Next question, "*What are the things in my life, things about my work, that I love? What has me turned on?*"

If you find it's a short list, or a list that's tough to get started on, maybe it's time for an evaluation, a checkup.

Maybe a strategic planning session with someone you admire, someone you consider a success.

Maybe it's time to take a hard look at what you're doing, or how you're doing it.

Just how "valuable" are you?

And how valuable can you become if it's
really important to you?
Are you letting the days and weeks slip by just putting
in your time? Or are you loving what you do?

CARPE DIEM.
What a great statement.

It's only a couple of words, but in any language it can't help
but add value to your day and to your life if you
adhere to the challenge.

Seize The Day, grab it, enjoy it.
Maximize it.

Throw your arms around each day and give thanks for
    big things, little things, and all the things you may
    take for granted.
Seize The Day with a zest and a zeal and a passion that
resolves to get the most from it.

I love how one of my teachers described it,
"*Wherever you are, BE THERE!*"
Squeeze every drop you can from the experiences you'll face today.
            Every day. And face the challenges head on.
        Don't shrink from them; attack them. Seize them.

The Bible, one of the all-time great books on wisdom,
also has something to say about how we should address the day...

The verse says,
"This is the day . . . .
I will rejoice and be glad in it."
Hey, now there's an affirmation for you.
    In the present tense, this day, every day, rejoice and be glad.
What a great decision to start every day with.

How do you suppose that might affect your attitude? Or don't
you give any attention to your attitude in the morning?

You know, so you'll start out each day already
    in the best frame of mind, just in case you run into someone
before you were ready . . .

Lots of people talk about needing their
coffee or caffeine to get them going . . .
    but don't neglect a little
rejoicing and gladness,
    looking in the mirror and
practicing your smile . . .
    any little thing that jump-starts your
attitude for the day.
It'll pay off in a big way!

"Nothing great was ever achieved
    without enthusiasm."

—Emerson

ATTITUDE IS A POWERFUL THING.

→

I'm sure you don't need me to tell you that one, but sometimes
it's amazing how you can overlook the obvious.
You don't miss many meals, or opportunities to feed your body, but
how often do you feed your mind? Did you know that you, yes you,
have the power to exercise your mind? Your incredible
thinking machine? There's a verse that says "*bringing
every thought into captivity.*" Wow.

Mastering thought, mastering the mind. Ever hear of that one?
A mastermind. Encouraging yourself, and becoming a master
of your emotions. Not being without emotion, stoic, or grim . . .
But knowing that as long as you get to choose . . . your attitude, or
what kind of day you're having, you will choose the positive.
     With empathy and understanding.
A great book to help you in that area is called
     The Greatest Salesman in the World. It's a little book you
could read in a couple of hours, if only you chose to do so.
     It's by Og Mandino, and it's not really about selling or sales
at all. It's about attitudes and life and understanding.
Every student, anyone who aspires to anything,
     anyone with ambition, or anyone looking for inspiration,
should read *The Greatest Salesman in the World.*

And then, periodically reread it
(remember that's how you really learn anything . . . with spaced repetition) . . .
For what it can do to remind you of building a foundation for
     your life.
For learning.
And how aspirations, inspiration, and ambition can propel you to
     incredible feats. History shows all of these to be the common
denominators of great accomplishments and uncommon success!
Sadly, in today's marketplace these seem to be in an all-too-short
supply. I first added this book to my library in 1988,
(I've added several copies since then) and recently reread it . . . again.

It is an amazing story on so many levels,
and Og Mandino is a master storyteller.
A passage from this book hangs on the wall of my office, and
hardly a week goes by that I don't pause and reflect on
the words in the frame . . .
If I feel depressed, I will sing
If I feel sad, I will laugh

If I feel ill, I will double my labor
If I feel fear, I will plunge ahead . . .

If I feel poverty, I will think of wealth to come
If I feel incompetent, I will remember past success

If I feel insignificant, I will remember my goals,
Today I will be master of my emotions.

You get the feel for this passage,
it's the journey to success that we're all on.
Somewhere along the way, wherever we are we could all use a
little encouragement. And then comes that day when you feel
you've arrived. Success. The look and feel and smell of success . . .
ahhh, finally. Even then you should consider, or reconsider, who and
what you are. How you got here and all those still on the journey,
and this passage reminds us of that very thing . . .

If I become overconfident, I will recall my failures
If I feel complacency, I will remember my competition

If I feel moments of greatness, I will remember moments of shame
If I feel all powerful, I will try to stop the wind.

If I attain great wealth, I will remember one unfed
If I become overly proud, I will remember a moment of weakness
If I feel my skill is unmatched, I will look at the stars,
Today I will be master of my emotions.

The scroll marked VI
The Greatest Salesman in the World
Og Mandino

YOU ARE TALENT!
You are talent-ED.

———————————————————————————————➤

Maybe no one's told you that lately, and that's too bad.
But I'm telling you now that you are a marvelous creation. You can
do amazing things, you ARE talented. You have *talent-S*, plural.
More than one.
Hopefully you know what they are. If not, make a list, go to work,
look for clues, ask someone whose opinion you respect.

What are your talents? What is your value in the marketplace?
That's what you're paid for,
THE VALUE. The value you create and bring to others.
And it does take time. It takes time to get better
and time to grow and time to bring the value. But
you're not paid for the time. It's what you do with the time.
How you convert that time into results.

About how much would you expect
you'd get paid for watching TV?
You might think it's big money with all the time most
people spend in front of it. 20, 30, 40 hours, or even more
every week.
We've got to look for better clues, be a better student than
buying into that plan for creating value.
What we settle for sometimes is disappointing,
but we can change. And that's the exciting part.
We can choose to become more valuable.
I grew up in an area where a large manufacturing plant was the
central theme of the economy. When business was good,
employees worked loads of overtime. And when business or orders
from customers were slow; these same workers were laid
off. Everyone talked about time-and-a-half
and overtime and lay-offs. And mostly I remember
everyone talked about how much they made "IN AN HOUR."
I make $5 an hour, or $10 an hour, or $20 an hour.

I never worked in that plant, though much of my family did and some still do. And there's nothing wrong with working in a plant or shop or whatever else you want to do to earn your living.

But you don't get paid for the time in that hour, or those 40 or 50 or 60 hours; you get paid for the tenure, the skill, the knowledge, the expertise . . .

THE VALUE you bring to that

company or organization in that hour.

Becoming more valuable is a pursuit of all Top Performers and High Achievers.

And the great part is, it's not just about the money.

It's about the "becoming,"

the rewards, the benefits, the quality of your life.

More. Bigger. Faster.
That's how we want it.
So let's fast forward.
Let's get better and get on the way to wherever it is you want to go.

Whatever it is you want to be. YOU CAN!
This is America! And you are amazing!

There are incredible stories of *uncommon success.*
Stories and maps and clues on how others did it. And you can discover them, if you're willing to continue

your learning. And become a student.

So go to work. Become a serious student for just a while

and explore the possibilities of increasing your value.

And what if *(can you imagine)*

You really did love what you do, or you were doing what you loved? How valuable could you really become?
Be on the lookout for little things that can change your life,

your learning, your ability to get better.
You still have to work at being a student, no matter your age.

Many people, especially young people, think that being in school automatically makes them a "student." If that were true, would being in a hospital make me a doctor?

Just because you don't have a job and you go to classes periodically, doesn't necessarily make you a student. Or mean that you're learning anything that you'll remember in a month, or a year from now.

You have to do your part.

Find out how.
Here we go!

WORK HARDER ON YOU

"Work Harder on You than you do on your job!"
—Jim Rohn

What does it mean to work harder on you than you do on
your job?

Lots of people work hard on their job. Not everyone
unfortunately, but let's say the majority of people do.
So that's common, working hard on your job.

Remember our purpose though, is to become UN-common.
A Top Performer. And that means working hard on YOU.
Improving your mind, your skills, your attitude. And as you do
these things, working harder on you,

how will your performance be affected?
How do you suppose you will do your job?
The same? No, you'll do it better, because

YOU are better. People will notice. You will become
more valuable and be better equipped to perform at a
high level no matter what your job is . . . today, and in the future.

Top Performers are uncommon. That's why they're
not in the middle, or average, or common.
Because they're at the top. They are continuous learners,

perpetual students of success, life, business, whatever.

Think of it as becoming the

"CEO of YOU, Inc."

You the corporation, all that makes up YOU. Life and business
and family and fun and accounting . . . the total package.
All the parts of your life are the various divisions of the YOU
corporation. And you,

as the CEO of YOU, Inc. are responsible
for overseeing them all.

How are things in the "family" division?

How about your "personal recreation" division of the company?

And are you showing reward and recognition to the "new members" of the corporation . . . your kids?

There's no one else to blame for what happens in the YOU corporation; you are The Chief Executive. How are you doing?

Your task is to give the necessary attention to all the parts of your life.

Some will be more demanding at times than others, just like the business world of doing your job. But you can't just focus on the division of "work" in the YOU corporation or pretty soon performance in the other areas of the corporation will suffer great loss.

Treat Life like it's your job

and then treat your job like it's . . .

just your job! *(not your life)* Ask yourself this question: *"What do I want to be remembered for?"* That one should make us stop and think *(something we all should do more often)* . . . "What's my legacy? What will I leave behind?

How will I be remembered?"

I heard a great analogy once from a senior executive on juggling the "balls of life."

Each ball represents a different area of your life.

Some are rubber balls and some are balls of crystal.

Not the crystal ball that you hear of someone looking into; no, these are balls made of fine crystal. Lead crystal.

Heirloom and keepsake crystal.

Some of those balls we juggle can be dropped or laid down for a while, and we can come along and pick them back up at the appropriate time.

But the fine crystal balls must be protected
>   at all times. These are the parts of your life that cannot be
dropped, cannot be left unattended.
>   These are the fragile parts of your life.
>> Your faith, your family and friends, your health.
Know the difference and respond accordingly.

Don't drop the crystal balls.

>   They can become shattered pieces of our lives that cannot
be repaired, or replaced. We can become so busy that we may not
>   even realize one of them is falling, or breaking, until it is
>   too late.
Only later do we realize they are lost, regrettably now, but still lost.

So pay close attention to all the divisions of YOU, Inc. like any
>   great Chief Executive would. Be sure to remind yourself
though, even those at the top can remain students.
>   In fact, that's where most of the best
>> lifelong students can be found.

"Don't bother trying to be better than
your contemporaries,
or your predecessors.
Try to be better than yourself."

—William Faulkner

I'VE GOT EXPERIENCE

I often speak to workers or managers or businesspeople who
love to trumpet their 10 or 15 or 20 years of "experience,"
and in some cases these are the individuals
who sit cross-armed with a little smirk, as if to say,
"What can you tell me that I don't already know?
I've seen it all in my career, I'm a pro, I've got
25 YEARS OF EXPERIENCE!"
And experience is a great thing, don't get me wrong.
But it's not the only thing, and it can't be something you
refer to as how good you were yesterday.

Let's suppose you were going in for surgery tomorrow, and the
good news is your surgeon has 25 years' experience.
It would probably be comforting that
you have an "experienced" surgeon.
But would you want this surgeon operating on you
with the same tools, training, and techniques
he or she used 10, 15, even 20 years ago?

Or would you want the very latest and greatest?
The newest technology, the best tools and training, and techniques?
The least amount of pain, the smallest incision,
the quickest and safest recovery?

Certainly the price for that surgery has changed in 20 years.
Wouldn't you hope there's been an increase in other areas?
Of course.

How ridiculous is it for us to think, in sales, or medicine, or any
other profession, that we can get by on experience alone.
Sadly though, that is exactly how many people think,
which of course makes it common.

What the marketplace demands is that you are
at the top of your game TODAY.
That you are better now on this particular
             project than you've ever been. That you've been able
to take all that you've learned up to this point
             and invest it in today. Experience alone is not enough.
You must continue to learn and improve.

How about this one:
"I can't believe I'm not doing better!"
(making more money)
             "I've got 15 years' experience on this job."
Sounds like something's wrong, doesn't it?
       Should you strike? How could a company do that to someone?

But after a closer look, here's what we find:
             someone who grew pretty well in the beginning.
             Someone who was excited about this new opportunity, who
threw themselves into it, learned what to do, and what not to do.
             In essence, someone who really went to work on
learning and improving in that first year.
And then the learning curve went flat.
And they just repeated what had been
             learned, what was easy, FOURTEEN MORE TIMES!

So it becomes not a case of someone with 15 years experience,
       but one year's experience, REPEATED over and over and over.
Stale, stagnant, not growing, not improving.
Sound familiar?

*"Remember not the former things;
       Do not dwell on what is past.
       Behold I am doing a new thing,
even now it springs up."* —Isaiah 43:18-19

You 6.0

If there are two or three or six versions of a certain software
or video game, which one do you want? Some might say,
"I'd be happy to have any," but the prevailing answer would be . . .
THE LATEST VERSION! Of course.
Sure, you want the 6.0 version, or Play Station 2 or 3 or 4
or whatever the latest, greatest, and best is.
You want to live in a place that is on the grow,
with new development, new opportunity. You move away from
stagnant or stalled growth to seek a better quality of life.
You read or research the best places to live, which offer you
the best of all that you seek for your life.

Don't you want the latest technology?
Don't you want the best from your towns and cities,
your transportation . . . why not the best you?
You would no doubt say, in all the things YOU want,
you'd choose the updated or the latest version.

Yet what you choose to bring to your career or company
or to the marketplace is the "outdated" version of YOU!
The skills or education or learning from times past. Choosing not
to continue to improve whatever it is you do or what you are, and
that means you're old news. Being passed by, or let go, because
the marketplace is choosing a later, greater version of worker
over your 2.0 skills or attitude.

Why is that?

Just too hard to update your "software," I guess. Just not enough
information available for me to get better in whatever area I
choose
I suppose.
*"And I don't have a computer at home, or books,
or encyclopedias, or trade magazines, or . . ."*

Hey, forget the common excuses,
find uncommon solutions.

How about scheduling some time at your local library?
> *"Man, do you how much they're getting for a library card these days?"*

Oh, that's right, it's free.
It's free, but you do have to go get it.
I know it may seem difficult, but you can do it!
> Be bold, march right into that library and tell
> them you want your very own LIBRARY CARD!

They might even give you one right there, now, today!
Books, tapes, computers, world wide web,
> all right at your fingertips. Imagine, your very own
> continuing education center.

Several years ago I heard a statistic that I could hardly believe,
> that only about 3% of America has a library card.
> Could it be?

Only 3%?
So I called the Library of Congress personally to find out.
> Though they didn't keep statistics on that particular issue,

we reasoned that it certainly must be less than 5%.

Hard to believe how we take our libraries for granted. But we
must have them, for our children to learn, right? So someday they
> can be as smart and as educated as we are, and far beyond.

In contrast, how many of us would you suppose have a
"video rental card?"
Would you say it would be more than 5%?
> Answer: without a doubt.
> Don't wait for the Library Channel to come to TV.
Go get the books and tapes and your ticket to greater success now.

We're so consumed as a society with "occupying" our time,
   being entertained rather than "investing" our time into learning
or taking our 2.0 skills to a 3.0 or 4.0 version. Sad, but common.

Uncommon says, "I will take advantage of every
opportunity to learn, to improve, to BECOME!"

"Sam was good 10 years ago, but you should see him today!"
"Susan started out as our receptionist, and today she's the C.O.O.!"
   COOL!

Continuing improvement is
   what you demand from the marketplace,
         and is also what the marketplace
                        demands from you.

Become uncommon.
Update the version of YOU!

The marketplace will notice the difference and
pay you well for it.

"When I get a little money
I buy books.
      And if any is left over I buy
         food and clothes."
                                          —Erasmus

WHAT'S SO GREAT
ABOUT "UNCOMMON"

Whether you're a student, an executive, salesperson, mom, dad;
whatever you are or you choose to be,
be . . .
Different.

A-Typical.

UN-conventional.
Be Memorable. And that means you'll

be unforgettable.

This is of course, just the opposite of common companies and
        individuals that are typical, or may even be called "average."
They just sort of blend in.
        Nothing wrong with that if that's your goal,
    but blending in doesn't make you memorable with
your customers or supervisors or teachers or co-workers.
In fact, it makes you forgettable.

How many companies have that quality in their mission statement?
        *"We just want to blend in with all the other service
providers and hope our customers like us the best."*
Conformity.   *(yaaaaawwwwnnnn . . .)*

Sound silly?
Why then do our companies think the thoughts and commit the acts
that are commonplace, the same, typical, comfortable, conventional?

Uncommon is different.

Uncommon companies and individuals . . .

Uncommon companies are the ones you've heard about.

Or will soon. In today's new economy *there's a whole new breed of uncommon individuals and organizations.*

Some have a unique identity that is instantly recognizable.
Companies like Disney, Ritz Carlton, Southwest Airlines, Federal Express, and countless others that bring about a mental picture of *"yeah, they're special."*
It's hard to describe any of them, what they do or how they do it, as common.

Uncommon companies are the ones you've heard stories about.
Or maybe you've even told stories about them.

About how great it is to work there, or how you were treated there, about the products or services they provide.
They really are different.
Distinct.
And because of what they do and how they do it, they've become
memorable.
And that's uncommon.

They've raised the bar.
And leaped over it. Raised it again and are in the process of more leaping.

There are any number of things that separate common companies and organizations from the uncommon, but I'll leave the long list to you and your investigative discovery process.

There are 4 keys that are found over and over in uncommon organizations.

THE KEYS TO AN UN-common ORGANIZATION

→

1. Vision
2. Powerful Communication
3. Action with Expectation
4. Celebration

That's the list. Short and sweet.
Sounds simple, doesn't it?
> The four *"common"* denominators of uncommon.
Let's look at each one.

Uncommon principle #1
Vision

The ability to look out into the future and see you and/or
> your organization doing something incredible. Vision says
> ## "that's where we can go;
> ### this is what you can become."

Lots of companies and organizations have mission statements,
> because someone once upon a time said they should.
> Then, mission statements were uncommon; now, very common.
Ever read one that sounded something like this. . .

"We strive to blah, blah, blah,
and serve our customers and blah, blah, blah . . ."
What does that mean exactly? What does it mean to workers
> and customers when they read your mission statement?

I was speaking at a convention in Las Vegas recently
to a group of entrepreneurs on the rules of engagement.
   We were discussing the rules of selling in this case, in fact the
differences in selling to women versus selling to men.

Whenever I ask the men in an audience, "What's the first thing
   that pops into your mind when I say, *The Rules of Engagement?*"

The list goes something like this . . .
War, Conflict, Battle, Military . . .

When I ask women the same question,
I get a completely different list.
Weddings, Brides, Marriage . . .
Why?
Simple.
It's the same challenge companies face every day in their
attempt to communicate with men, women, new employees,
         tenured workers, customers, prospects, and
other individuals inside, and outside, the organization.

It's The Rules of Engagement.

It's communication, but its all over the board. And that's not
where companies and organizations want to be if THE goal is
         to be uncommon.
We want a vision. Clear-cut.
   It's not a mission statement so much as a purpose.
         Or a place that everyone can see, know where we're going
and understand how we'll get there.
It's a powerful thing, and it's of course, uncommon.
      ## How do you get your vision?
         Your idea of what you or your business will become?
Lots of ways. But you have to be paying attention
in case one of them tries to whisper in your ear . . .
         "here's your vision."

Walt Disney used to go with his daughters to an
amusement park outside Los Angeles on the weekends.
He loved the carnival atmosphere, the music, the smells,
    kids laughing, it was a place he loved coming back to
again and again.

One day when the merry-go-round stopped, he saw up close
for the first time one of the "tricks" of the trade.
    Only the horses on the outside went up and down.
The inside rows were bolted to the floor, which was
        dirty and unkempt, much like some of the other
    areas around the park. And he saw the horses were
old and fading with paint chipped away.

Can't you almost see him that day, taking a pencil and paper from his
        pocket and scratching out the words,
        "No chipped paint. All horses jump."
Bang. A vision begins.
Disneyland and the Magic Kingdom are born.
Wow!
    Vision is a common denominator of all
        uncommon organizations.
Then comes the communication.
Or for the uncommon, POWERFUL communication.

Can you imagine Disneyland or the Magic Kingdom becoming
    what it is today from just a few words on a piece of paper?
Amazing, but Disney still had to communicate his vision.

Can you see his first visit to the bank to explain what he'd be
doing with the money he was asking for? It's not like taking a
    banker out and showing him acres of orange groves
        would help him see
what Disneyland
        looked like in Walt's mind.

It was most certainly a challenge,
even to the most powerful of communicators.

Uncommon principle #2
Powerful Communication

Companies *(and relationships)* live and die on the strength of their
communication skills.

Issues like attracting the best candidates, training and
continuing improvement with workers, interdepartmental issues,
unions, stockholders, trust, morale, retaining the best talent . . .
and that's just for starters.

If you were to address a group and say to them, "We're going to
discuss

the art of communication,"

what's the first thing that would come to mind for most of them?

The ability to . . .
Speak.
That's it. Communication is the ability to speak, to speak well,
to be eloquent, wax poetic, blah, blah, blah . . .
Is it?
Let's have a look.

While managers and workers alike often agree
on the need for better communications,
few really understand what it is.
Here's a question for you,

Does communication
prevent miscommunication?

Think about it for a second or two, don't answer just yet.

Does communication prevent miscommunication?

Sorry, but it doesn't. In fact, in many cases it causes or at least
contributes to it. It doesn't solve anything or bring us
closer to a solution. It doesn't always improve the situation,
but in some cases can actually make it worse.

It's rules of engagement, all over the board, different messages
to different individuals. Not where we want to be,
yet all too familiar territory.

Common.

So what's a company to do?
Better objective for better
communication . . .

SEEK FIRST TO UNDERSTAND

→

Everyone wants to be understood.
    It's the number one basic human need. Not to be
loved, though that's high on the list, but to be understood.
    Interesting . . .

Your objective in becoming uncommon is to
    adopt the *"you go first"* philosophy.
Hey, we all want to be understood, but you go first.

When this is the position you take, now you climb into
the driver's seat in the communication process. You become a
    more powerful communicator because you understand what
needs to be addressed, and maybe even how you need to address it.

It's not your ability to speak but your ability to understand that
    makes your communication more powerful. In all my years
        in the business and profession of selling, it's amazing
    how many people think sales is about talking.

Talk talk, tell tell, talk talk. If I can talk enough, you'll buy.
And of course, the top performers in sales know
    that's not at all what sales is.

So while communication doesn't prevent miscommunication . . .

does understanding prevent
mis-understanding?

And the answer is, by definition, absolutely.

It's true for workers, customers, leaders, teachers, speakers,
parents and spouses: better communication comes from
    a greater understanding, and it makes them all better
        in their relationships and better at what they do.

So if your goal is uncommon and powerful communication, you must learn to ask better questions on your way to a greater understanding.

Ask BETTER questions.

You have always known how to ask. You learn it as a child.

"Mom, can I have . . ."

But when you're 30 years old and asking the girl of your dreams to marry you, or asking for the order to make a sale, you can't ask the same questions you did when you were seven.

Or to put it another way, you can't stay in grade school.

That's why they make those desks so small.

My second grade teacher was Miss Eula Belle Appleton.

I loved Miss Eula Belle, and I loved second grade.

I was entrusted with the special assignment of hall monitor at lunch and recess, a "personal assistant" of Miss Eula Belle. I'll never forget coming home that year with my report card and asking my mother what that "promotion" part was all about.

"You'll be going to third grade next year," was her reply. But I didn't want to go to third grade.

I loved it in second grade with Miss Eula Belle.

I was somebody in second grade, and I had a good handle on what it took to be a successful second grader. But alas . . .

You can't stay in second grade forever!

Seems lots of workers and salespeople try it just the same. Their questions are stale and tired, often few and far between. The goal must be to get better at asking.

If you want to read some good books on questions
        try Matthew, Mark, Luke, and John.
        It's four different accounts of many of the same stories
of one man's life.

This particular individual really knew how to ask questions.
    He also delivered some powerful presentations using
something called "parables."   Memorable and extremely effective.

You know the saying about two ears and one mouth?
Listen twice as much as you talk and all that? And as corny as it may
    sound, it's true. YOU TALK TOO MUCH!

And what's worse, you're probably talking too much about things
        the other person has no interest in! They don't care!
But you keep talking anyway, you'll turn that prospect around, you'll
talk your way into this sale, or make your point in this discussion.

Amazing.
Just imagine you're playing the lead role in a "sales movie"
    (no, not Death of a Salesman*)* and the person
        sitting across from you is, what else, THE DIRECTOR!
Take your cue from him, he will tell you
    what you need to do for a successful performance.

How about these questions?

Do you ICE skate?

What makes you angry?

When was the last time you cried,
        and for what reason?

What was your first
childhood job for money?

What are some of your favorite foods?
How do you face a new day?

What 5 movies would you like to see again?

In a word or two, describe how
    you would enter a crowded room.

Who would ask questions like this?
Ringling Brothers Barnum and Bailey Circus.
On the job application for
    the position of Clown.

Why would you ask those questions?
        And if you did, would you suppose you'd gain
            a greater understanding of that individual?
        Asking better questions is, you guessed it, uncommon.

When combined with vision,
        powerful communication
is a force that propels individuals and
        organizations to places they've
            never been before.

WE CHOOSE . . .
TO GO TO THE MOON

When President Kennedy gave that famous speech in 1961,
it shook things up. In Washington, in Houston, in Congress,
    inside NASA, across America, in Russia, and around the world.

Without a doubt, it was a bold statement. And he could have
    had a consensus agreement with his proclamation
had he not added the next line . . .
"We choose to go to the moon *in this decade!*"
Bang!
What?

By putting a time frame around his vision of the moon,
    it redefined everything. It was not enough just to go,
we had to go now.
    Or at least begin to go now.

Even though the space program was already in existence
    in some form, at some level of success, we were certainly
        trailing at the time in the race for space. But that day,
    everything changed.
The challenge was new.
And it spurred new ways of thinking, new ways of seeing things,
and new ways of believing it could actually happen.

Hmmm. Uncommon?
No doubt.

As I recall that speech went something like this . . .

"We choose to go to the moon in this
decade and do the other things . . .
not because they are easy,
but because they are hard!"

Wow!

Because it was hard.

Challenging stuff. Is that what you're focused on?
New challenges and inspiration for yourself and others
to do something incredible.

Is that what YOU'VE CHOSEN?

Choose to do something today
that some may say is impossible.
Don't make small plans; reach for the high bar.
The view's much better there.

Uncommon principle #3
Action with Expectation.

It was vision, powerfully communicated, and a call to action with
giant expectations that landed us on the surface of the moon.
"One small step for man . . ."

Faith and Action, with an expectation.

It's one thing to take action.
Just be sure to double-check your definition of action.
We've all seen lots of people on the job or in life
doing things daily that it would take quite a stretch
to define as action.

If I asked you to name 3 leaders in your organization, could you?

Who comes to mind? What are some of the qualities or clues to success you would find in them? Leadership is critical to uncommon. Leadership.

That sometimes means less management, even though there is a place for management. But leaders and managers aren't the same, there's a difference. Organizations, to be successful, need managers. Someone to be responsible for the books, keep an eye on the money, reporting, organizing, controlling, etc.

But somewhere in an organization there must be a leader, or leaders, if they are to reach the status of uncommon.

Leaders are necessary to gather a group and point it toward a "common" or shared goal or direction. Everyone must believe *"we can make it,"* that together we can get there. It creates teamwork, a bond, and it creates a momentum or inertia that propels the group in the direction of their goal or objective. That's leadership.

"The will to do, the soul to dare."
—Sir Walter Scott

One of my favorite leadership quotes is from Benjamin Zander, the conductor of the Boston Philharmonic Orchestra. The leader of a music-making organization.

Can you imagine a manager conducting the Philharmonic? Just making sure all the i's are dotted and the t's are crossed? That's a tough one to envision. A creative and uncommon organization absolutely must have leaders. True leadership that encourages growth among individuals and the whole of the organization.
To pursue dynamic improvement and achievement.

"I set as the goal, the maximum capacity that people have. I settle for no less. I make myself
a relentless architect
for the possibilities of human beings."
—Benjamin Zander

Leaders aren't just at the top of an organization. They can be inside somewhere, at almost any rung on the ladder. Too many individuals think *"Oh, what difference can I make in my position?"*

Leaders begin to develop their leadership qualities right where they are. Generals weren't always generals, and CEOs were in the mailroom once upon a time. Don't fall victim to *"Oh yeah, if I were a vice president, I'd make some changes around here . . . "* C'mon, get started, change what you can where you are.
Change you.

The story of David and Goliath is well known.
Most people think the real message of that story is how David, a little shepherd boy, went out and won the victory over this battle-tested giant.
But if you go back and read that story again, there's a greater message in there. Can't you just see David going in to the king and announcing his intentions to go out to this battlefield and face Goliath?

Can you imagine the stunned looks
he must have gotten? The surprised responses?
"David, what are you thinking?
You're five foot nothing, a hundred and nothing!
And Goliath is, well, a giant! He's big, he's wide,
he has all these weapons and knows how to use them.
What could you possibly be thinking?"
And David replied,

"Is there not a cause, I will go!"

Is there not a cause?
What's your cause?
There was a vision, and David had captured it. It was a cause he
obviously believed in and it drove him to do something
very uncommon.

He became a leader
right where he was.

There's ancient wisdom that says if you're good with the small
things, you get a shot at the bigger things. But you have to begin.
Like the message that says *"You don't have to be great to
start something,*
but you do have to start something
to be great."

Uncommon can be that simple; just start. Just choose to begin.
Begin, and the law of inertia gets on your side.
(Did you know inertia is a law? You'll read more on this later, but
inertia says *a body in motion "tends" or has a tendency to remain in motion.)*

So get going and watch what happens.

Of course, don't neglect the expectation, or faith.
The believing part of achieving.
It's a big part of the uncommon equation.

Uncommon principle #4
Celebration

> ## *"Celebrate what you want to see more of."*
> —Tom Peters

This is one of the most neglected, and maybe the most misunderstood, principles of uncommon success. Be a good student, and you can find the celebration example all around you. From sports champions to Sea World to NASA. If that sounds a bit odd, follow along on this one.

I won't bother with the sports part of celebration. Watch any championship competition and you'll witness a celebration by the winners.

Basic principle of winning . . .
Don't neglect the celebration.

Basic principle of corporate America . . .
We don't have time to celebrate.

Hmmm, what's wrong here?

I love books. *(allow me to wander just a bit)*
Not long ago, in a used bookstore, I found a gem and bought it for **one dollar.** The title?
"Tigers, Trainers and Dancing Whales."

Intriguing, huh? I was relatively sure I could learn something
   from a book with a title like that. And I was right.

What I learned was that the uncommon principle of celebration was
         the standard method of teaching and achieving at
Sea World and other animal attractions.

Ever wonder how those whales dance?
Or how in the world they can get those dolphins to come flying
   out of the pool right on cue?

Pretty simple, really.
When the instruction for our water-loving friends begins,
         they are asked to jump over a rope in the pool.
      Guess where the rope is placed for the first attempt?

Not on top of the water, but underneath the water.
         At the bottom of the pool.

         Dolphin swims over the rope . . . gets a fish.
         The dolphin may barely understand at this point
what's going on, but gets a reward for the desired result.

So, over the rope again . . . and another fish reward.
Then, you guessed it, raise the rope.
         Still no problem, over the rope, get a fish. This continues
         until the rope is raised out of the water and our young
student must actually come out of the water to get the reward.

No problem still, for dolphins have that ability. To jump out of the
water. It's not even that difficult, once they understand they can.
   Fly over the rope, get a fish. Then there's clapping and some
verbal celebration . . .

   "Way to go, whatever your name is!"

Whether a few inches or several feet, the behavior is reinforced until finally the rope is removed. The behavior though, continues for the fish "celebration" and on to the next trick.

Of course, how we'd do it in Corporate America would do it is jack that rope
30 feet up in the air and scream at those dolphins to

"get up there and I'll give you this whole bucket of fish!"

And if they didn't immediately respond by flying to their goal, there might be some yelling and screaming and reprimanding
and some other type of hardball tactics, just so they'd know that the boss isn't playing around.

Sound ridiculous?
Sure does. But it happens daily. Very few managers ever learn the power of celebration and reward because they're not open to trying it, for whatever the reason.

And of course, celebration worked for NASA.
When we got to the moon, we stuck the flag in, hit a few golf balls, beamed video around the world and said
"Hey, look at us . . . here we are on the moon!"
We should all celebrate the power we have to make innovative and dramatic change in whatever it is that we do.
The good news?
You CHOOSE.
To get better, or to go to the moon.
Major principles of uncommon?
Vision,
Powerful Communication,
Action with Expectation and Celebration.

See how it works for you.

PASSION.

———————————————————————→

Add this word to your vocabulary, and look it up in the dictionary.

I know you think you already know what it means,
   but look it up anyway. Guess how many people look up words
in the dictionary? Would you say it's a common occurrence?

Right, uncommon. So do it.

Passion is one of the clues to uncommon.

It's been said, and I believe, that great dancers aren't great dancers
        because of their technique. They're great dancers because
of their love for dance, their passion for what it is they do.

Same for you. Whatever you do, have at it.
        Fast Forward.
Wherever you are, be there!

Whatever you do, passion adds to the art.

What are you passionate about?

"Life is either
a daring adventure,
        or nothing."
                —Helen Keller

MARATHONS AND RACES

What's the difference between a marathon and a race?

Think about that one for a second . . .
   How many winners in a race?
When I ask that question to a live audience it doesn't take long for
   someone to shout, "One!" That's it, one winner in every race.

How about a marathon?
Why do marathoners run? To finish first?
        Some people say a marathon is just a long race.
    Twenty-six-plus miles . . . wow.
How many winners in a marathon?

Would you guess more than one? Without a doubt!
Anyone who competes, certainly anyone who finishes,
   considers it a personal victory. Why is that?

That's great student stuff.
There are great life lessons in there somewhere,
   on preparing, training, focusing, sacrificing,
   and finishing the course.

I have a friend who is a runner.
Jim is president and CEO of a business machines company.
   He is passionate about many things, including his business,
and he loves to run. I mean, he loves running. He loves thinking
about running and discussing running and even preparing to run.

He's a subscriber to all the runner magazines and has
runner friends and really studies the art of running.

Jim is passionate about running.

Jim has competed in a variety of runs including marathons, like the Kiawah Marathon outside of Charleston, South Carolina, where Jim finished first in the over-40 division. *(Jim would want me to remind you that he has just recently qualified for that over-40 age group.)*

And he finished 17ᵗʰ overall out of 2,400 runners.

Jim trained seven months,
almost every day, for that run.
He calls it his greatest athletic accomplishment.

This from an all-conference running back who's had 90-yard touchdown runs and 400-yard games. He's had
baseball successes and has played golf all over the world.
But when Jim hurt his back, it wasn't his golf game
he missed most, it was his running. I'll never forget sitting across from him at his desk and listening to the passion in his voice as he talked about his preparation and his next run.

It seems he's almost always in training for that next run.
Jim is highly motivated to set a personal best in his next marathon.
It might be slightly different from a personal best that you or I would consider.
His goal?
To finish 26.2 miles in under 3 hours!

If you do the math on that one, it's an incredible pace.
Something tells me Jim will check that goal off the list one day.

And while that big wooden pelican sits on Jim's desk
marking his accomplishment for that day at Kiawah,
there were 2,399 or so others who, by their finishing,
or maybe just participating, also consider themselves winners.
It's an amazing thing to witness a marathon firsthand.
At first glance you might not think so, but allow me to share a story about one of my marathon experiences . . .
as a spectator. Albeit an active spectator.

I happened to be in New York City on the first day of November in 1998. I was in town for a conference, and that Sunday was a day free for enjoying the city. When I realized that this was the day of the famous New York City Marathon, I decided to spend my afternoon exploring a 26-mile adventure that is the ultimate challenge for thousands of runners of all ages. And to do something uncommon,
to capture a special memory of this day.

I had bought a hardcover book from a street vendor.
It was a pictorial of New York *(one of those souvenir books),* and after watching a bit of the runners on the marathon course I got the idea
to get my book from my hotel room and have
these marathoners sign it as they came off the course.

It was amazing.
To see these runners from all over the world pushing through the final few hundred feet of this historic course and literally collapse after crossing the finish line.

Many friends and family members were there to comfort and congratulate and carry away these combatants, these victors.
Each runner was wrapped in a thermal blanket, and as they passed by me in various stages of exhaustion, I asked as best I could *(many obviously spoke no English)* if they would sign my book.
Sometimes just extending the book and the pen
was enough for them to understand what I was asking.

This was their moment.
And it was being captured, if only by someone
they didn't even know. You could see their eyes light up as
they were being asked for an autograph like some celebrity
or sports hero. Many were amazed at the request,
but most all signed, happily. And congratulated me on a great idea.

It was a fascinating sight.

As best I could, I asked where each was from . . .

Atlanta, Boston, Baton Rouge.
San Antonio, Chicago, and LA.
Australia and Alberta.
Brazil, Holland, Venezuela, and Mexico.
England, France, Switzerland, Germany, Japan, and more.

Many wrote little asides or humorous lines or even an occasional
    message of inspiration. But the best of the day was
    from a gentleman who had to be in his sixties and maybe even
        a member of the over-70 division.
Inching along the sidewalk, drawing on every ounce of his strength
to make his next step, and surrounded by his family who were
    almost carrying him in their arms, he summoned them to stop
and took my pen to write these words . . .

"There is but one freedom, man running along.
        And the courage it takes to be there."

And then he signed his name, which if I could make out
I would happily share with you here. I don't know where he
        finished in the marathon that day in New York,
but I will always remember him as a winner.
What a day that was, made a more memorable experience for me
    because it was shared with all those passionate performers
from around the world who rose to this challenge and won.

Don't fall into the trap of comparing yourself to someone else,
    on the job or in life.

Compare yourself to the potential inside you.
To dare.
To try. To attempt something incredible and see it through.
    Something that you and others will never forget.
Try being better than you are now and see what can happen.

In life, as in a marathon, there is no limit to the number of winners. By choosing to participate you have taken a giant leap from the ordinary into an extraordinary journey. Stay the course, press on!

As I watched those runners come through Central Park on that beautiful autumn afternoon, I thought about so many things.

But at the top of the list was just this . . .

Life is Good.

Go for it. Drink it up. While we still can.

"You can't start over in life's marathon. You often can't choose your circumstance or situation. But you can choose your attitude . . . discipline, work, training, victories, and disappointments in life teach us some of our greatest lessons."

—Bob Bardwell, *wheelchair marathoner*

LADIES AND GENTLEMEN, START YOUR ENGINES!

I was discussing my speaking services and availability with a senior executive of an organization when he confessed he'd been less than bowled over by some of the company's recent lack of success with their choice of speakers.

He remarked in a bit of a dead-pan manner,

"The last thing I need is another motivational speaker!"

To which I responded,

"There are no motivational speakers.
Only those who can
inspire others to motivate themselves."

Most individuals and organizations don't understand the difference.

Inspiration and Motivation

What's the difference? BIG difference.
It's the difference between inside and outside.
Take a look at these two definitions . . .

1. Inspiration . . . inciting action, cause, inducement, purpose
   CAUSING MOTION!
A reason for doing something.

2. Motivation . . . the act or power of arousing the mind or emotions,
an agent or influence,
to give inspiration to.

Some people say Zig Ziglar, or Michael York,
    or maybe the president
        of your company is a "motivational" speaker.
But we can't be motivational *to you!*

That part of the success equation can only come *from YOU!*
The only one who can *Motivate YOU is YOU!*

*That's why the ONLY kind of motivation is
SELF-motivation.*

By definition, motivation is a reason for doing something,
    while inspiration is an outside agent or influence that gives you
        the INSPIRATION to take action.

That means there's really only one kind of motivation, and that's . . .

What causes people to do incredible things doesn't come from
        outside, it's something internal. A force that drives you to
go somewhere, become something, achieve a goal, survive in extreme
conditions, or overcome adversity.

A leader or mentor is a big part of that process, the inspiration part,
    but the rest is still up to you and me to motivate ourselves.

We have this corporate obsession with management.
There is such a management mentality,
        and yet such a lack of understanding
for what it really means to move people or propel a
    group of people to accomplish great things.

I spent many years in "management" primarily as a sales manager.
I have always preferred "Director" to manager;
    as in Director of Sales,
        Director of Advertising or Regional Director. It creates a
mental picture for me of an instructor or coordinator or even
    a conductor, as in the conductor of an orchestra.
        Why can't we have more of the
            uncommon, "non-managers" who really understand
            how to move people to a desired place or result?

You can aspire to something greater than
management alone.
To have a greater impact on
people, to bring out more in them,
        to allow them to discover their greatness in
        whatever they do.

Or better yet, whatever they really desire to do.
    Growing people is the greatest opportunity for
        growing organizations and growing profits and
growing something that's more valuable than money.

Leaving something long after you're gone.
A legacy, or even a legend. Something that you or your group
    or company or organization is known for.

Wow! That's uncommon.

What if you were to aspire to direct?

The way a director moves stars and cast in a movie to an
award-winning performance that will be seen and discussed
    as a classic example of his craft.

I have a young friend, Mark,
who, at an even younger age, decided he wanted to be a director.
   A filmmaker. He simply chose to move his learning and
interests and aspirations in that direction.

I have known Mark and his family since he was in grade school.
   He made many "short film" projects on the way to shooting
and directing his very first movie,
   while he was a senior in high school!
   I was at The Manor Theater to view firsthand
      the celebration of opening night.
Family, friends, newspaper story,
   vehicles from the movie . . . it was quite an evening.
And it was a cool movie, starring Mark's classmates in a story that
Mark had written himself. Somewhat out of necessity I suppose,
   since to direct a film you must first have a story or script for it.

Mark has been a student of film and his craft for many years now,
which may sound strange since he is just a college student today.
   And while that doesn't make his age a strong case for his level
of expertise, there is little doubt in my mind that you will hear of
      Mark again one day. I believe he will become
   an uncommon filmmaker in the very near future.

For many reasons, but largely because one day he
decided to. And began to pursue his goal. It is evident to
anyone around him his passion for the art, and his aspirations
to be a director.

Godspeed Mark, see you in the movies.

Leaders are directors;
encouragers and conductors who direct a group of individuals,
      coordinating and crafting those individual
performances to blend seamlessly together to produce a
masterpiece of music, or film, or results.
What if you could be more than just a manager?

What if you could instruct and inspire as true leaders do with their words and deeds? By coaching and encouraging to accomplish something incredible?
You can.

You may not be a powerful speaker, but by your actions or encouragement or accomplishments, you can inspire others to give more than they ever have. To do more than they've ever done, or ever thought possible to do. Much of it is changing the way you think, and the way others think about you, themselves what they do, and how they do it.

Leadership, true leadership, is an amazing thing. How one individual can have an impact on how others think, act and achieve is powerful.

And we've already decided, leaders are wherever you find them. You can be a leader right where you are. Be known as a leader, as someone who can be counted on. As an example to others.
As someone with an attitude and aptitude that is uncommon.

Be more than just a manager.
Strive to be a leader or director or conductor.

People will notice.

"To be both a speaker of words and a doer of deeds."
—Homer

KNOWING THE LAW
(and using it) and how it can absolutely work for **you.**

How well do you know The Law? Or "the laws."
No, it's not a question about constitutional law or trial law,
I'm speaking of the laws that were established
thousands of years ago.

Natural laws, laws of creation, God's laws."

Stephen Covey refers to some of them as "The Laws of the Farm."
The first time I read Mr. Covey's reference to those laws
I had to say "Wow!"
I'd never thought about it that way, but it was true.
Anyone who's ever been on, or even around, a farm knows that
some basic fundamental truths are always at work.
Amazing, but then after all they are "the laws."

There are several that we could talk about here, but I'm only
going to cover three of them. These laws are POWERFUL and
predictable. They work, because they are THE LAW!

• The Law of Gravity
• The Law of Sowing and Reaping
• The Law of Inertia

There you go. Three fundamental basics of Life, and you can find
all three right out there on the farm. I should mention that I had
the opportunity to observe these principles, firsthand
*(different than laws . . . some laws can be principles, but not all principles can be
laws. Got that?)* since I spent much of my first 18 years on this earth
on a farm. That's right, cows, chickens, tractors, outdoor
plumbing, the whole farm experience.
It was not exactly the "pre-Beverly" life of the Hillbillies,
but at times it was close.

I did see plenty of "the law" in action though, and I have seen those
        same laws prevail in the years since leaving the farm,
    in business and in life. Let's look at each one.

Number 1
The Law of Gravity

This one's a no-brainer, and really I just threw it in
        to prove my point on laws 2 and 3.
    Trust me on this one, if you drop a bale of hay out of the loft,
it's headed straight down, but fast! And that hay looks so
        light and harmless when its growing in the fields.

By the same token, when you're at the bottom
        trying to throw that bale UP TO THE LOFT,
    you can really feel that gravity law at work.

So I don't expect to have to debate the law of gravity with anyone.
On the farm, in the city, even in some parts of outer space,
        gravity prevails. Why? Simple. IT'S THE LAW!

Number 2
The Law of Sowing and Reaping

I can understand how some people might have a problem with this
one, but not only is this one of the ancient "wisdoms" of the ages,
            it's a law of the farm and it's been the law
    for thousands of years.

You don't have to live on a farm to know that
            if you plant beans you get beans,
        if you plant potatoes you get potatoes,
            and if you plant tulip bulbs,
provided you get that miracle of the seed, and the seasons, the sun,
and the rain . . . all working together BOOM you've got tulips!
    It's The Law!

You know how it works.

You don't plant beans and get tulips!

And you don't put out onion plants and get tomatoes!

No, it just doesn't work that way. And it's been going on like this for several thousand years that we know about.

I and thousands, maybe even millions like me, have also found that this law works for emotional growth, spiritual growth, and yes, even personal and professional growth.

You really do reap what you sow.

But not today or tomorrow. Nope, on the farm, and in life, it takes a little time. You plant in the spring, and nurture *(feed, water, study, love, whatever you use to nurture)* for a season *(like summer)* and then go into the fields at harvest time.

Then comes winter, and after that you regroup and grow all over again. On the farm, you never stop growing.

WOW, did you get that? What if we're all like that?

We never stop growing!

Never stop learning, studying, getting better, becoming more valuable. For ourselves and for others.

On the farm that's the way it is, but in life it's up to you to make the growing continue.

If you want to reap more friends, sow some seed. Smile, listen, be a friend and in due season . . . bang!

You'll have more friends. It's got to work. It's The Law.

*"It is never too late
to be what you might have become."*
—George Eliot

And finally,

Number 3
The Law of Inertia

This might be my favorite.

Even though I really like the reaping part on number 2.
The law of inertia is one of those you may
  not have learned on the farm, but you should have
    learned in school. It simply states that
A BODY IN MOTION TENDS TO STAY IN MOTION!
(that's the good part)
    AND A BODY AT REST TENDS TO REMAIN AT REST.
(not necessarily a good thing)

What law could be simpler than that?
It's the old "snowball rolling down the hill" concept.
    The "rolling stone gathers no moss" script.
        It means also that if you'll begin any task, no matter how
difficult, just begin *(try doing it for 5 minutes)*, then inertia's law will
move you in the direction of completing that task.

And if you do it for 5 minutes and begin to feel the law working,
    5 becomes 10, and 10 becomes 20 and soon you've gone
        several times farther than you first anticipated because
    you *"tended to remain in motion"* in the direction of
completing the task.

It works the same way for your goals. It's awesome!

Use it as your secret weapon.
It's INERTIA, and it really works, because,
well you know . . . it's The Law.

LIFESTYLE

I've been fortunate to have some great teachers on lifestyle.
In my estimation, at the top of that list has to be Jim Rohn.

"WHAT IS *YOUR* STYLE?"

When Mr. Rohn first asked me that question in 1988,
I wasn't sure how to answer.

I wasn't prepared to define it or defend it, much less improve it.
Lifestyle is something you cultivate. Cultivate, now there's a
good word. It means, after the farm references of course,

"to improve or develop

*by careful attention, training, or study: devote time and
thought to; to raise, or produce."*

Cultivate.
It takes a while to develop LIFESTYLE. But take it from me (*and
Mr. Rohn*), it's worth it. Cultivating lifestyle is a little like
building equity in your home or refining something over time.
A fine wine or a valuable antique that only gets better with age.

Lifestyle is how you enjoy what you have in the pursuit
of whatever it is you want. Some people think, again,
it's about the money.
But it's not. You can get maximum style with a little money.

You might need some other ingredients though, like creativity.
Of course, if you have plenty of money you might get by
being less creative. You can just pay someone to be creative,
or to assist you in developing and enjoying
the style of your life.
Do you get it yet?

It's not the amount that determines the style, *you* determine the style.

And if you use that style to increase your value,
you guessed it, it usually leads to greater financial rewards.

Lifestyle can be the way you dress,
      what you do to relax,
   how you get away from the pressures of
every day, making time for your spouse or kids.
I've always said parents can never know when some regular old
   ordinary day becomes a day your child will never forget,
         just because you did something with them.

I've had my son say, "Dad, remember the time we did . . . "
And I might vaguely remember coming home tired and beat but
   took the time to invest in him, and that small amount of time
became the most valuable part of that day. Because 5 or 10 years
         later, he still remembers *that part* of that day.
         Don't neglect cultivating style in
         your life. It's not the amount, it is the style.

If you think about it, it's really hard to talk about
personal development without getting, well,
      personal!

So you'd have to think a book on personal development would
contain some very personal elements . . .
and you'd of course, be right.

"No pessimist ever discovered
      the secret of the stars, or sailed to an
      uncharted land, or opened a new doorway
for the human spirit."
                              —Helen Keller

FAITH

I don't know where you are in the spiritual part of your life,
but surely by now if we're any kind of student at all, we've come
to the conclusion that human beings are complex creatures.
We have so many levels and layers.
We're intricately created.

The Bible describes you as being *"wonderfully and fearfully made . . .
in the very image and likeness of God."*
And if you do your part in the student department,
you come to certain conclusions in the characteristics,
or makeup, of your beings.

There is definitely a physical man *(woman)*, an emotional self,
a thinking or mental makeup, and yes, a spiritual aspect
of humans that makes you unique.

I won't get into this much deeper than to say this is an area where
you should pay careful attention.
It's easy to get "faked out," to gather information that may be less
than "The Truth." And any good student in search of clues to
success should pursue as their ultimate goal of understanding,
The Truth!

That is the way you should approach your investigation in this area.

For my part, in my 40-plus years of study,
I have come to some exhilarating conclusions.
Revelation information.
Life-changing inspiration and instruction.

And I'm only too happy to share that
with other students of life and success.
Students just like you. I teach a class every week,
and have now for the past eight or so years, about this very thing.
About the instruction and inspiration and examples
of spiritual growth and improvement.

Most of our classes are about life. Enjoying life.

Long life, really long life, and how certain principles can take us closer to, or farther from, our long-term objective.

It is truly fascinating.

I encourage you to look into books that have something to say about not just the fads of today, or short-term pleasures,

but that set a standard, outline a plan, and give certain steps that anyone can take to enjoy a

long *(and I mean longer than you might even imagine)* life.

The best book I've found for this type of study, hands down, is the Bible.

You can learn so much from this collection of books and writings that have been around for thousands and thousands of years. Surely that alone must intrigue you to want to know more about those examples and plans and principles that were set long ago and endure even today.

Don't trust your feelings or preconceived ideas you may have about this; be a good student and find out for yourself.

One of the most powerful pieces of instruction I've found in that book is on Faith. And Faith is necessary for us humans.

Oh, I suppose you could get by without it, but it would no doubt be a less than fulfilling existence.

Why, you say? In a letter to the Hebrews, one inspired writer put it this way, *"NOW, Faith . . ."*

There's a little more to it than this, but that is always such an encouragement to me and others. Like, OK, here's Faith, now.

Wow, I've read it literally hundreds of times and it's still great reading.

Ever have a book like that? Or a story you just never get tired
of hearing or telling? Me too, and this is one of those.
So to continue,

"Now, Faith is the
substance of things hoped for;
and the evidence of things not seen."

Hey, that's powerful.
If you've ever hoped for anything,
Faith was a part of that.

The substance of things hoped for. You were exercising your Faith
and maybe you didn't even know it.
That second part's not bad either, evidence!
We all understand what evidence is . . . right?
In a courtroom, it's offered as "proof."
Proof of something we can't yet see; that's evidence,
that's Faith.

"Faith is the daring of the soul
to go farther than it can see."
—Unknown

If you ever start a new business, you'll be putting Faith to the test,
believing things will work out, hoping for success.
If you seek a better life, Faith is part of the hoping equation,
and even better, evidence of things to come.

I've heard the stories from my elders and my contemporaries,
about mustard-seed Faith
(you don't need much to do great things apparently)
and about the kind of Faith that moves mountains.
I love William Blake's words on this one . . .

"Great things happen when men and mountains meet." Wow. There's a challenge right? So put some study time in on this one to see how you may be better equipped to understand and maybe help the process along a little. It's worked for me and for thousands upon thousands of others for several thousand years. Why not you?

In fact, in that same letter to the Hebrews the writer gives all these incredible examples of how Faith played a part in historic, monumental triumphs for a long list of "rock-solid" individuals.
Check it out.

And don't forget about the action part, the work.
That's your part.
That same ancient script says that Faith, without works, just doesn't make it. It's dead.
So don't neglect the work,
it's the second half of the Faith formula.

"The most rewarding things
you do in life
are often the ones that
look like they cannot be done."
—Arnold Palmer

THE ABILITY TO FOCUS

On the wall of my office is a calendar.

No big deal.
    Many of you have the same thing on the wall of your office.
But this one's a *"motivational classics"* inspirational calendar,
        which might be my favorite of all the specialty calendars.

It has a big image of something colorful,
breathtakingly beautiful, majestic,

    you get the picture. Then it has a subject or title for the
        month's lesson, and then a quote, caption, or phrase
that lights your fire.
I love it.

One day around the end of the month, in fact as I recall it was
maybe the 27th, I'm sitting at my desk when I get this urge
    to get up, walk over to the wall, and turn the calendar
        to the next month.

Now there's still a few days to go in the month, but I convince
myself that I may as well get a jump on next month now
    and turn the page.
        I had been in the throes of making a difficult decision,
one that would definitely have a major impact on my career.

So I walk over and turn the calendar to the next month.

I'm met with a full-color close-up of a bald eagle,
    his golden eyes seemingly fixed firmly upon mine,
        the title in big bold letters proclaimed . . .

"FOCUS:"

(which at the time seemed to be something I'd been struggling with)
And just below it read,

"If you chase two rabbits, both will escape."

BANG!
Message to me, get on with the decision, Fast Forward.
Focus, pick a rabbit, then he's yours.
You just never know when the little things you surround
yourself with can make a difference in how your life works out.

I suppose I could have gotten some important life message from a swimsuit calendar, but . . .

nah, never mind.
Focus.

*"Creative thinking involves Imagination.
And imagination is
more important than knowledge.
For while knowledge defines all we
currently know and understand,
imagination points to all
we might yet discover and create."*
—Albert Einstein

JOURNALS

Let me encourage you to keep a journal. In fact, keep several.

My journals have become somewhat notorious in our family. I have written in and given them to my wife, son, daughter, mother, brothers, nieces, and nephews. Also to friends and business acquaintances and even people I didn't know all that well.

Some of the stories and correspondence that has come back to me because of those blank books is amazing.
Someone always jokes that on special occasions, birthdays, anniversaries, Christmas, or other events,
someone's gonna get a journal from me.

At graduation I gave "another" special journal to my son, and
so she wouldn't feel left out, one also to my daughter.

My mom happened to be at our home at the time, and Lindsay laughed as she opened the firm, square, book-shaped present . . . "Guess what this is," she laughed.

"How many journals do you have now?" her mother asked.
"At least 10 or 12," she said.
"And how many does Dad have," I asked?
"Probably 50 or 60" she joked.
But I began counting them up and at that time that was pretty close.

I keep journals for lots of things.
Business, ideas, instruction, records, daily entry,
big days in my life, even golf and fishing journals that have
my writings about great rounds on great courses or
about that 12-pound bass I caught, what day it was
and what the weather was like.

I should mention that my goals journal is bigger than
my golf journal, so don't lose your priorities.

Some days are just too important to trust to your memory.
And the great thing about these writings, when you read about
them again, it's like throwing another log on the fire of your mind.
Suddenly the flames blaze, and the fire of that memory
burns almost new again,
allowing you to vividly recall that special day or event.

Journals are a very special part of my library.
Why is it that every home worth more than a couple hundred
thousand dollars *(you know; quarter-million, half-million, million dollar homes),*
all have studies and/or libraries in them?
Doesn't that sound like a clue to success?
A key to uncommon?

I once heard someone say of their massive display of books,
"No, I haven't read them all, but
I feel smarter just walking into the room."
Wow!
An environment that makes you feel smarter, or more creative,
or makes learning more attractive.
Wouldn't that be something we'd all want?

. . . AND I QUOTE

Oh, I almost forgot.
In any library, one *"gotta have it"* is a book or books on quotations.
Great words of inspiration, instruction, humor,
deep thoughts, it's kind of a *greatest hits* collection of
wordsmanship! *(I'll explain this a little later in the book.)*
I think that's my word, not that I'm trying to take credit for it . . .
In fact, I hope you can see throughout my books and
tapes and seminars,
I'm usually trying to give away credit.

That's one of those foundational principles we talked
about earlier.

The Ancient Books have something to say on that subject also,
"Give honor to whom honor is due."
I have found that to be a "rock-solid" principle to put into practice
   in all areas of life. Try it!
And since we're discussing it, throughout this book
   you'll find just a few of my favorite "greatest hits" quotes.
When you read them, focus on them for just a
   moment or two and reflect on their meaning . . . to you.

Because sometimes the meaning of a quote hits you full force,
   and you get it, bang! But then there are times when you take
the words and roll them around for a closer look, or listen quietly,
   to glean the meaning of the quote and how it may apply to you.

The other reason is to hopefully interest you in
the wisdom of others to the point where you'll add several
   quote books to your new library.

Review the quotes of famous people who were faced with much of
the same adversity and many of the same challenges that you and I
   are confronted with today. And the great part is, even if
   the words were delivered hundreds, even thousands of years ago
   they are just as powerful today.
I challenge you to be a student of greatness; in your personal life
   as well as in your profession.

*"One machine can do the work of
50 ordinary people,
but no machine can do the work of
one extraordinary person."*
—Nido Qubein

CREATING VALUE THAT LASTS . . . FOREVER!

Often when I speak to live audiences, I ask them a question about
  this kind of value. So let me ask you,
      "How'd YOU like to create value that lasts forever?"
In just 5 minutes?

Sound like it might be hard to do? Nope, just the opposite. It's easy.
Easy to do, but easier not to do . . .
    so you know what the common choice would be, right?

How can you create value that lasts forever in just five minutes?
three words . . .

Hand written note.
(I know hand written note is technically two words, but humor me.)

That's it.
Sorry if you were expecting thunder and lightning and a booming
revelation . . . but when you write handwritten notes, a powerful
    thing happens. First, someone gets a message, maybe of
encouragement, and how many of us could use one of those today?

Or a message that says "I'm thinking of you."
Or "I appreciate you" or even *"I love you."*
    Ever write a letter or send a card to your mom or
maybe your grandma?
    And then she opens it and reads it and throws it away, right?
You know better.
She reads it and then she SAVES IT. She keeps it.

When I was away in the Air Force in 1975, I wrote to my family,
mostly because we were told to write to our families . . .
      by our caring sergeant and training instructor.
      We thought it was a good idea too, so we ALL wrote
letters home in the evening during our basic training.

Guess what my grandmother did with those letters.
Right, she read them and showed them to her friends and then
    saved them in a shoe box. Can you believe it? She saved them.
Several years ago my grandmother passed away.
    What do you suppose happened to the letters?

I got them back.
And how long will I keep them?
Until I can pass them on to my children . . .
they'll last forever, because I choose to keep them.
        They're something special that many years ago,
    took me only a few minutes with pen and paper to create.
Powerful.

Who needs to hear from you today?

Just a note to your Mom or Dad, sister or brother, son or daughter,
        or nephew . . . or maybe a love note to your spouse.
    Try it, it works.

It can even work today with a less than personal mail, email.
    I get email from lots of individuals that I save, even print out
and keep in my journals, just to go back and read
        in case I'm having a tough day or week, or to remind me
            why I'm doing what I do for my living.

Like to hear a couple?
I have to warn you,
    they make me sound pretty impressive . . .
They're encouraging, and some are hilarious.

A personal note can still be personal, even if it's sent electronically.

"Dear Michael,
    Thanks for being such a special speaker at our convention . . .
By the way, I bought my first journal and started in it December
12th. No sense waiting, I had things to say . . . Jackie"

Having an impact on someone's life is an amazing thing and an awesome responsibility when you think about it . . . and I do, a lot.

"Michael,

Happy Monday! I wanted to thank you, not only for your message and encouragement, but for your example of excellence . . . Kenny"

You never know when some little thing you might say leads to inspiration and life change for someone who's really listening . . .

"Dear Mr. York,

I really enjoyed your session with our leadership team . . . something you mentioned inspired me to dig out an old atta' boy letter of mine . . . and when I did, something amazing happened. I felt like I had just received it, even though it was several years old . . . it means more to me today than when I first received it. I have it up in my office and am changing my environment . . . thanks for the charge, I'm re-energized and ready to go.   William"

I get the opportunity to speak in jails from time to time, and prisoners get the same message as executives or other students.

That personal notes are powerful, and I know they're listening because I get mail from them almost every time I speak . . .

"Mr. York,

Thank you for taking the time to come and speak to us. It is not everybody that will give an encouragement to people like us who've made the wrong choices. Please continue to share your encouragement with those locked up, it really helps . . . thanks, Earl"

And even personal mail from around the world.

Like from my Ukrainian friend Yaroslav, who came to Charlotte on a business trip and met his future wife before returning to his home country. We spent some time in "coaching" sessions, and he was an eager student.

I came across his address weeks later and dropped him a note.

His response is a treasure and I keep it to this day . . .

"Hello dear Michael,

I have no words to express my joy
because of your letter!

Of course, I do still remember our lessons and
meetings . . . of your speaking business, I have no
doubts you are the best in it and all your competitors
can only enviously look up at you from the deep bottom
where they sit comparing themselves to you . . .

write me please when you have the mood for it.

Your friend, Yaroslav"

My friend Yaroslav,

and a friendship that continues because of a personal note.

What are you doing in the next 5 minutes?

JOURNALS II

Here's a couple of added-value items on your quotes
  and notes and writings.
  Keeping a journal is uncommon.
  I cannot stress to you enough how important
  this area is, not only to top performance in your
career, but preserving something even more important in
almost any area of your life.

Physical, emotional, spiritual, personal, family, relaxation,
  recreation; they're all areas that make up an
important part of just who it is you are, and they help to track
your progress or important moments in your life along the way.

There are lots of great reasons to have a journal.

Journals are kind of like those potato chip commercials.
You know, you can't have just one.
  If you get started putting your
    thoughts, ideas, special moments that you want to
    remember on paper, or even more important, special
    thoughts and moments you want someone near and dear to
    you to know and remember . . . amazing things happen.

Here's another *"gotta have it,"* you absolutely have to try it.
It's another example of that law of inertia we talked about earlier.

I've been keeping my journals for over 15 years, and
  I wish I would have started much sooner.

My kids have been writing in their journals during much of that
same period, so now at ages 21 and 19, they've been keeping
  written records of special times in their lives for well over
HALF THEIR LIVES!
Wow.

Is that exciting to you?
That you, or maybe your children could take their special
    memories gathered up over a lifetime and

invest them in tomorrow!

That's a life lesson that I was able to impart to them almost
30 years faster than I learned it.
    That's exciting to me.
    That we can teach, prepare, and equip the next
generation years and years faster than we learned these things.

"What if I'm not a writer?"
I've been asked that one before.

Or maybe you don't feel like you can keep a diary.
    It doesn't have to be a diary, you don't have
    to make an entry every day. But don't let a year go by
without making an entry about a special memory or special day.

And you don't have to be a writer.
Although keeping a journal will absolutely
sharpen your writing skills. Think of it as just keeping notes.
    Anyone can take notes.
You've done it before *(hopefully),* at one time or another.

Just keep all of your life notes in one book for starters,
your journal. Then you can add a second or third for work or play
    or whatever else you want to make notes about and keep.

You'll be amazed at the value you can create with
    good notes on life's lessons and learning. Just put it there in
your journal, and you'll know where it is.

When you want to refer back to it, no problem, it's available.
    It's so much easier than tracking down all those legal pad
    notes and files, and loose leafs . . . then you won't be asking,
"Now where did I put those notes?"

My Own Personal
Sampler

What could be so special about keeping a diary or
writing in a blank book?

I can see how you might be asking that question,
especially if you've never tried it.

But without me going on and on about the merits of
keeping a journal of your own, and just so I can give
you an idea of how it spills over into every
area of your life, here's a

glimpse into my private pages.

And just a few of the entries I can relive
each time I read them again.

From one of my very first journals . . .
*"Wow, this is a big journal, and only $3.99 for a book with
no writing. A blank book.*

*But by the time I write only a few pages, it will have doubled or
even tripled in value. And one day when I, or Sandi, or Ryan, or
Lindsay should read this . . .
it will be priceless! Not for sale at any price.*

*How amazing, that we can create value in a blank book, or in us;
becoming a better person or better husband or father. Better leader,
speaker, writer, or whatever it is we wish to become better at.
Adding value seems to be a worthwhile endeavor."*

(Journal Entry: March 22, 1996)

"Today I had lunch with Lindsay. Not unlike times before when I've had lunch with her or Ryan. I remember going to school to surprise them for lunch.

I don't do it nearly as often as I should, but I do think about how special all the times that I have are. This is one of those 'first things first' days that lets me show my family just how special they are to me.

Some people might think there's lots more important things they have to do than eat lunch with their child at school. Oh, there may be more 'urgent' things, but how could this lunch on a day like today not be the most important place I could be. I love you Lindsay.

Dad"

Journal entries are powerful.

They can be about lots of things.

They can be instructional or recreational.

 This entry was made on one of those recreational afternoons . . .

"The mountains of North Carolina are beautiful. And so is my wife. So this day is a special one that lets me enjoy the beauty of them both. Walking around this small mountain village with this beautiful lady on my arm.

Looking in all the shops and enjoying the cool of the day with Sandi. Lunch at a quaint little place and a stroll through the park. Just a day trip a couple hours away from home, but an afternoon with my sweetheart to always remember."

Sometimes you get the opportunity to encourage friends or acquaintances, or even family.

Here's an entry from one of those days . . .

"Got a call today from my brother, who was without encouragement. Which is a difficult place to be. So I encouraged him and encouraged him to start a library. To begin to study, plan, and set some goals.

So I'm sending him this library start-up kit, of sorts. Including Stephen Covey's '7 Habits,' a journal, a dictionary and the 66 books of The Bible. Not a bad start for any library."

I've kept many journals and entries for my son,
and here's one of those . . .

(Journal Entry: May 28, 1999)
"Ryan. My son.
Today I will give you this journal. I have kept it, and my thoughts and memories of you in it, for almost two and a half years.
I wanted you to have it on the day you graduated from high school. Congratulations.
I pray that you will always be a student.
I love you son, Dad"

Don't trust your memory . . .

" . . . reflect on days passed. And on the things that contribute to the fullness of your life. And never underestimate the power of words. To inspire, to create, to move. To heal or to hurt, to witness, to correct, and to convey your love to one another . . .

The more you read, listen, and write; the more you'll read, listen, and write. One day you'll know what I mean.
In celebration of the power of words."

Michael York

So there are just a few of my personal journal entries. Hopefully you can see how powerful it is to reflect on those special days, special times that you don't trust to memory. They're written down. So I can pull them from the shelf and live those moments all over again. Take good notes from your life and make your blank books "priceless."

Give it a try, and see how it works for you.

"I'm just a regular guy who happens to do something pretty well. Everybody does something well. Everybody!"

—Mark Martin, *NASCAR driver*

DAD, THE COACH

Another part of my life that has been so fulfilling has been
    as a coach. Like many dads, I helped with
        pee-wee league baseball and Cub Scouts and volunteered
    my time to increase the value of children's experiences and
help them learn about life through sports and activities.

To learn the worth, the value, of belonging to something bigger
than any individual . . . a TEAM!
It was something that my dad and other adults taught me as a
    young boy, and I couldn't help but give something back
        when my son came along.
But I wasn't exactly prepared for what came along in 1995.

Ready For a Challenge?

I've always loved sports. I love competition.
    I love the participation, and I love to witness
        those battles of competition. I've played one sport or another
for most all of my life, but for the past several years
        I've been able to participate in another way.
As a coach. It's taught me a lot, and I've enjoyed being a student.

Both of our kids have been fortunate enough to attend a wonderful
school for the past several years. The first year they attended there,
        one of the administrative staff had seen me coming
    to Ryan's games, and he was the coach of both the junior high
        and varsity boys' basketball teams.

In the spring that year he asked if I would be interested and available
to coach one of the school teams the next year. I said sure, thinking
        I'd be handling maybe the junior high or junior varsity teams.

"I'd like you to coach the varsity high basketball team,"

he said. I was a bit stunned and felt much too unprepared
to coach a high school varsity team.

It was a very young program going into a new conference,
not to mention the fact that it would be a formidable challenge
    for me personally.

I accepted.

That first year we were out-manned *(if not out-coached)*
in most every game. We went something like 1 and 14.
The one win though, is a game that is still talked about to this day.
        In fact just last week the mother of one of the players
    on that team called me to get a copy of the game video.

Having lost to the same opponents by 20 a week earlier, we
finished the rematch with an overtime period that saw the game
end with our team on the floor consisting of only three,
that's right three, players.

Three on five at the final buzzer.

        Most teams couldn't finish a fast break with a three on
        five, but we finished a game . . . and won.

There's more to the story, of course, but we went from
        that kind of beginning to a season five years later that ended
            in the state tournament as an at-large bid.
        That was most likely my swan song.
What a great experience.

Adding value to the lives of dozens of young men.
Teaching, coaching, studying, listening. I'm not sure who learned
    more, them or me. I knew soon after I took the position that
        I had to go to work on becoming a coach.
And I was able to get the books, make notes watching other games
and other coaches, and make the process pay off as a win, win, win
all around.

One of the greatest things
(and at times the toughest) during that time was coaching my son.

My dad coached me as a youngster, and that was special for me.
Thanks Dad.

Ryan and I had lots of pre-game, post-game,
and during-game chats. There were some incredible wins
and some heart-breaking losses.
When we started our player-coach journey together, I knew
from experience that it would carry added pressure for him.

Some people would inevitably say things that might be painful
to hear. Things like the only reason he's playing is
because his dad's the coach.
I challenged him to practice with a passion and
a purpose that would help him to arrive at a place where,
whenever I took him out of a game, people in the stands
would wonder why.

To be so valuable a performer that he was obviously one of
the best players on the floor, no matter who was coaching that
team.

And he did just that.
He didn't start his freshman year, but came in as a sixth man.
A shooter.
And he was.
A picture-perfect form of an outside shooter.
(OK, maybe I am a bit biased, but I am a coach.)

In his sophomore year, he was not only a starter but voted
by his peers the MVP of the team.
As a junior he set a number of school records including
most points in a season *(404)*, most 3-pointers *(56)* and
was again voted MVP and First Team All Conference
by the coaches in the league.

He capped off a great career with a senior season that saw him
eclipse the 1,000-point mark and again receive MVP
and First Team All Conference honors.

Wow. Did he ever meet my challenge.

He grew his game and his leadership to the point that he
shouldered much of the responsibility for how the team
performed, good or bad.

That's quite a load for a young man.

So why do I share this with you, what's the relevance?

2 things.

1. It's my book and my son.
     *(So I get the chance to be **"Who's The Daddy"** proud of the boy.)*

2. It's a great life lesson.

It doesn't always work out that way: boy works hard,
     shoots for hours on end in the driveway,
sleeps with one of his dozen basketballs,
develops pure-as-the-driven-snow shot, sets records,
          scores bunches, wins awards.

It didn't happen for me.

I loved the game, but a great shooting night for me was anything
over two points. Ryan averaged over 20 a game for two seasons.

Certainly there has to be **a measure of talent.**

But passion, desire, persistence, determination, and practice
     all play a part. And it's a great lesson,
especially for a young person, to see that pay off.

I'm so glad I could be a part of it, up close and personal.
     As we sat side by side on the
          bench after his last game and the rest of the teams had left
     the floor, the crowd filing out, we reflected for a moment
over those 72 games.

Four years.

We laughed a little, and even got a little misty-eyed, but we both
knew we'd been a part of something special between not just
     a coach and a player, but a dad and a son.
          And I'd had the best seat in the house.

It was one of the most special parts of my life so far.

Along the way Ryan became a better life student and continues
his learning today as a positive role model off the floor.

I would have never thought it possible to have fit in those
72 games over those four years *(not to mention all the practices)*
with my work schedule off campus.
Head Coach.
Wow, amazing.
Look for opportunities to do things in your life that give you
fulfillment, satisfaction, joy, and lifelong memories. It may
even be something that you see as difficult or impossible. But
seldom are the things of great worth easy to come by.

Accept the challenges, confront the tough tasks,
consider the possibilities. After all,
you miss 100% of the shots you don't take.
(If you ever become a coach, feel free to use that one.)

Another reason I share the story of coaching Ryan is because
it didn't take long for the coach/player relationship
to come full circle.

Not long after, in the midst of starting my own speaking and
consulting business and going through the rigors of lifting
my enterprise off the ground, I was going through
some difficult decision-making on the direction of the business.

Financial issues and the day-to-day grind that begins to wear
away at the fabric of even the strongest of individuals.

I came home in the afternoon and my wife handed me
a letter from Ryan, who was away at school.

"Ready for some tears?"

she asked. A bit puzzled, I opened the letter and read . . .

Dear Pops,

I wanted to thank you for your card the other day, and just for some other stuff. That card really got me thinking just how much I appreciate you, and love you.

First of all, I wanted to thank you for being a father who taught me how to be a man. Not just a man after excellence, but a man after God's own heart. Your integrity and character . . .

When you made the decision to start your own business, no one believed in you more than your son. And that still holds true today. I was listening to your CDs the other day, and it got me to thinking . . .
"Hey, Ryan, wherever you are . . .
BE THERE!" Wow . . . so simple, yet so profound.

In my life I gotta grab hold of every day, and love every minute of it. Mr. Frease (the Dean of the school) said something in class the other day. He finally found out that I was only 19, he couldn't believe it . . .
"Man, this boy must have one good teacher." . . . it started me thinking, yeah, I owe a lot to my Dad. I want to thank you for that.

Now, I don't love you because of your business, or your character, or your success . . . I love you for one reason, because you're my Dad.

I know I've never written a letter quite like this, but I thought it was time I told you, in a real in-depth way . . .
Dad, I'm so proud of you.
I think this is the first time I've ever told you that, but definitely not the first time I've thought it . . .

You are a good Dad, I just wanted to tell you. I just wanted to encourage you to keep going. Your stuff works, it's good.

Hey, I know you have rough days, but hey, that just means when you make it big, you've got the goods, you overcame it all.
Here's a verse for you, Proverbs 24:10 . . . (don't do this)
"If thou faint in the day of adversity, thy strength is small . . .

Hey, I miss you a lot, I'll be home in 6 months . . .
I love you Dad.
Ryan Michael York

Wow.

One of the most powerful lessons of encouragement that I've ever received.

From a 19-year-old "teacher" who remains
    one of my students and a student of life.

It is a powerful thing to have a child, or any individual
    teach you lessons that you once invested in them.
I pray you will know that power one day.
Thanks Ryan.

I remember after one of those tougher-than-usual losses,
    riding home in the car trying to think of something, anything
    to say to my son to ease the pain . . .

"Let's not talk about the game," I said.
        I put my arm around his shoulder and said softly,
            "How about tonight, I just be the dad."

Sometimes we should skip the lectures,
drop the critiques and the coaching, and not be what I call
"a master of the obvious."
I'll give you a real-world business example.

A one-time VP of sales I had, would on occasion call me to get a
firsthand report on how sales were going. He could skip all the
        pleasantries and go right to the main event, *"What's doing?"*
or "Where are we?" meaning what's the number. Or sometimes
he'd just say, ## "What's the number?"
Then if we were anywhere south of our sales goal, it would
    draw a response like, "Huummmm, that's disappointing."

No kidding.

We were about ready to pop the champagne.

Come on. Masters of the obvious aren't the most visionary people
you'll ever be around. They're predictable. Obviously.

"I play a lot of cards . . . obviously."

—'Lenny' from *That Thing You Do,*
(one of my daughter's favorite movies)

Then of course, there's the call after we had made goal.
Congratulations? . . . Way to go? . . .

Great job?

Nope.

Maybe an acknowledgment of sorts, and then,

"So where are we on the next project?"

Never once in two years of working with this VP did I ever get
one personal note, even though we set 9 of the top 10 record months
in the company's history while I was there.

It would have been easy to do, but it was

easier not to do it.

Other things going on more important I guess.

Don't let that be the case for you or your company.

If you're in a position of leadership,
convey to the rest of the team that they, individually, matter.
That you notice when they do the job well.
Or when they achieve at a high level.
You'll be amazed at the response you'll get in return.

Take the time to recognize and encourage people,
or your children, or your spouse or your friends.
Know when to turn it up,
and when to dial down the questions and advice.
Sometimes you may just need to be a dad, or friend, or mentor.
An encourager.
Or just someone who understands.

We all need that from time to time.

COOKWARE ON THE HOOD OF A CAR

My Story

Let's skip the real early stuff and pick up
the story of our hero in 1988.
It was, in many ways, one of my toughest years.
I was trying to carve out my niche, somewhere between
corporate America *(where I had had some success)*
and the entrepreneurial world of owning my own business
(where I really wanted to succeed).

Financially, times were tough, but it was during this time
that I made some of my greatest discoveries.

(Flashback . . . 10 years)

It was 1978. I had just taken a new bride *(not that she was different
from my old bride; she was, `er is, my only bride . . . love you honey).*

After going into the Air Force right out of high school, I was
back where I'd been 3 years earlier. Young, with little experience,
and even less money. I found a job at a radio station
that started me at $88 a week
(they obviously didn't realize at the time just how valuable I was . . .),
and I began my new life as a husband and provider.

I still remember Mr. Paul Slatton, a gentle giant of a man, looking at
me over the top of his glasses and his deep, raspy voice announcing,

*"If you last for a month
I'll give you a $25-a-week raise."*

And true to his word, he did.
After a few weeks of this, I answered a little classified ad that read,
"$100 a week. Part-time, work 3 nights a week."

Now that's about what I was making working ALL week long,
so even I could figure out, this would be a good thing.
    So with the enthusiasm that cannot be dampened by ignorance,
        I headed for the interview at a local hotel.

There must have been a hundred people that day
who wanted to make $100 for a few hours work.
    I took a seat down front and when this tall dark-haired
gentleman took the platform he immediately grabbed my attention.

He was well-dressed, with a sort of *"Business-Elvis"* look,
    and a voice that could melt butter in that classic southern
drawl. I was one of the volunteers for a presentation that day, one
of maybe four or five in that hundred-or-so audience.
    Chuck Ray struck me as a successful businessman and speaker,
        and told us only a handful of people would be right for
    this opportunity, and he'd give us a call if we were the one.

Sure enough, I got a call. Chuck asked me to come in.
I did, and the rest, well, that's for another book. I began learning
    about SaladMaster cookware, found out about a guy named
        Zig Ziglar, and set my feet on a path that would lead me
    into the world of selling.

I should also tell you that Chuck was nothing if not
passionate about his craft and his product.
    I can still remember riding to those dinner demonstrations all
around Florence, Alabama, in that gold and white Lincoln Chuck
had earned from the company. And the looks, laughs, and stares
        we used to get at stoplights.
    It just might have had something to do with the hood ornament
on that Lincoln . . . a 1-quart saucepan. SaladMaster, of course.
    To this day, Chuck's the only guy I've ever known
        confident enough in his own style to drive around
            with cookware on the hood of his car.
Thanks Chuck!

MEET JIM ROHN
(FAST FORWARD 8 YEARS)

In 1986, I met Anthony Morris. A friend and fellow pursuer of
the Great American Dream. Tony was a great friend and influence
on my entrepreneurial development. Not long after we met
he began to share what he'd learned, and introduced me to some
books and tapes from a businessman by the name of Jim Rohn.

I hadn't heard much up until now about anyone like Mr. Rohn,
other than my exposure to Zig which had, like my sales career,
been sort of on-again, off-again.

But Mr. Rohn gets much of the credit as the teacher that
swept me off my feet of uncertainty and helped set my sails
into the winds of change.
Shakespeare once said,

> *"When the sea was calm, all ships alike
> showed mastery in floating."*

Wouldn't you want to find out who's for real behind that wheel
when the wind begins to blow? And I did.

I became a navigator, determined to find that destination where
I belonged. Mr. Rohn was a mentor who affected my life,
as well as my career, and he remains that today.
My bank account didn't reflect it till years later, but the
impact was immediate, and the change in me continues even today.

Lots of speakers talked about sales and motivation, but his
encouragement about things like
building your own library,
taking and keeping lots of pictures, and especially
the writings of a personal journal, were small seeds that
found fertile ground deep inside me.

It gave me new insights into many things.
One of the most revealing was that for the first time I understood
   a part of my grandmother. She was always collecting things
and pasting pictures. Clipping and writing and collecting.

Books, diaries and journals, cards, letters, and more.
   All this time I thought she did that because she was old and
didn't have anything else to do. How naive I was. Now I
      understood, she did it because it was important.
   Maybe most important for her to leave something for us
long after she was gone.

Thanks Mr. Rohn.
And thanks, Grandma Hattie.

Now I understand.

LIFE IS TREMENDOUS

It was about this same time I met a man by the name of
Charlie Jones. I heard Charlie at a national meeting
of top performers in Dallas, Texas.

If you were a dynamic speaker, you might think you'd need a name
somewhat more memorable than just Charlie Jones.
Charlie was, and he did. Charlie was tremendous . . .
I mean *TREMENDOUS!!!*
Everyone called him Charlie *"Tremendous!"* Jones.
You have to do it with caps and exclamation
marks and bold or italics.
You can't just write it, like Charlie didn't just speak . . .
He *SPOKE!* With a supercharged energy and excitement
that was bigger than any room he happened to be in.

Charlie "Tremendous" Jones gave me his book that day,
"Life is Tremendous." It's one of those small books you
can read in a day, and of course I did. It's a lot like Charlie.
It seems to bubble up and spray right out of your hands.

And it, too, speaks as much to the way we live as the way we
work—
How he worked at being a husband and father in
giving value to those around him.
I still take that book out and read through it from time to time.

On the first page, it says . . .

"LIFE IS TREMENDOUS!

It really is.

You can be happy, involved, relevant, productive,
healthy and secure
in the midst of a high-pressure,
   commercialized, automated, pill-prone society.

It's not easy, nor automatic, but it's possible through the development
of certain personal qualities which make up
   the traits of leadership. And you can be a leader, because leaders
are made, not born.

Are you ready for leadership?
Whooooo, let's go!"

And then, as only he can, he signed it to
"Tremendous Michael & Sandi, 2 Timothy 1:7
Charlie 'Tremendous' Jones."

Thanks Charlie T!

By the way, it's OK to write in your books.

In fact, I encourage it. Write in the margins, at the top or bottom,
things that you want to remember or things that you think of
   when you read something in the book.
         That makes the book even more valuable, because now it's

a collaboration between
you and the author.

And in my case *(and most cases)* what I write is a collaboration
between me and another teacher . . .
   now we've got a regular mastermind group going.
                     And all because you weren't
                     afraid to write in your book.
I should mention that it should be YOUR book.
Don't write in a library book or a friend or co-worker's book.
   If you're going to interact with the writer . . . buy your own copy.

Everyone Should
Write a Book

When I first began to write this book it seemed as many
challenges have: easy, yet difficult.
Imagine . . . ME, writing a book. An author. Wow.

Can you imagine YOU writing a book?

I remember hearing a writer say everyone should write a book.
If only for the experience of having done it.

So over the past 10 years or so I have kept notes and journals and
scripts and clips and ideas so that some day
    I could pull them all together and have a collection
        of what I've learned and taught.
    About sales, about life, and about getting better.

To share with you now, that collection.

My notes and life lessons on becoming more valuable
    in the pursuit of something, of anything, that's important to you.
    And to demonstrate to all of my teachers that I have
        made a concerted effort as a student.
That I have paid attention, and kept good notes.
And that their investment in me has yielded a measurable return.

It is an exciting adventure to accept

    the challenge of doing something better tomorrow than you
can do it today. And tracking your progress, proving your
improvement with notes and results.
It's like Mr. Covey's "Seek first to understand." It's not the norm.
        Oh, I know it should be, but it's behavior that's atypical.

It's uncommon.
        Not typical, not normally what we expect or receive.

Everyone wants to receive value, everyone wants to be understood;
    But be on the lookout for your chance to be valuable.

You can absolutely stand out as one of the most understanding,
value-giving persons that people know. And you'd better believe
it makes them appreciate you, even gravitate toward you.
        Children want to be like you,
            men admire you, women love you,
    light seems to radiate from . . .
            OK, OK, sorry, got a little carried away.

But you know what I mean. People are attracted to you
because you're different,
in a good way.

If you give value in building any relationship and try to understand,
    before you're understood,
you'll definitely be on your way to becoming uncommon.

*"I give value first
        and I have fun every day."*
                —Jeffrey Gitomer

MAKE YOURSELF AVAILABLE . . .
to opportunity and life change.

⎯⎯⎯⎯⎯⎯⎯⎯⎯⎯⎯⎯⎯⎯⎯⎯⎯⎯⎯⎯⎯⎯⎯→

One of the most truly uncommon individuals I have had the pleasure of learning from is Jeffrey Gitomer.
Jeffrey is one of the greatest marketing geniuses I have ever met. He is widely known as an authority on selling and sales skills.
And for teaching most anyone willing to learn

how to be better at the profession of selling.

Jeffrey's column, *"Sales Moves,"* appears in business journals around the world, which is where you'll often find him, speaking to aspiring sales professionals and business leaders.

I met Jeffrey at a Chamber of Commerce meeting soon after moving to Charlotte, North Carolina, in 1992. But it was an impromptu meeting in the airport several years later that had a major impact on my future and what I do today.

After sharing some basic *"How's business?"* comments,
I mentioned to Jeffrey how I admired what he'd accomplished and that my goal was to one day be a full-time speaker and trainer.
Jeffrey looked me right in the eye and said,

"Michael, you've got to do it . . . NOW! Go for it!"

It was the right message at the right time. *What was I waiting for? Was I on some 20-year plan to becoming a speaker and doing something I'd always known I wanted to do?*

It was my destiny.

And I knew it.
So on that night I stopped becoming a Director of Sales for a publishing company and began to pursue with a vengeance, building my speaking, training, and consulting business.
I wouldn't actually make the transition until a couple months later, but mentally, that night I became a professional speaker.

It was a defining moment.

One I had prepared for since I was a three-time 4-H club public speaking champion in the eighth grade. Years of selling and reading and speaking and training had taken me to this point.

But sometimes it takes a spark of encouragement or inspiration at that precise moment to propel a career or a life toward something new and incredible.

And that was the moment.

Jeffrey has a style that is beyond imitation.
He is certainly one of a kind. I'll never forget one of
his first critiques of my platform speaking . . .
"You've got to make major points faster!"

Great advice, to platform speakers
or aspiring sales professionals or almost anyone.

His book *"The Sales Bible"* certainly does not need
my endorsement, but I recommend it to you here anyway.

It is a powerful book that will absolutely change how you think about sales and about becoming better in almost any area
that requires creativity, marketing, and positioning
yourself as different.

Over 150,000 copies of this book have been sold. Wouldn't you
like to know what over 150,000 highly motivated selling
professionals know . . . that you may not? It's available.

Are you?

Thanks Jeffrey.

CONTINUING IMPROVEMENT

It's one of the clues of success and definitely uncommon.

"Never let formal education
get in the way of your learning."
—Mark Twain

Education and imagination can exist together.
Edison and Einstein are two great examples of educated learners
with a powerful curiosity and creative imagination.

America was founded by opportunity-seekers and risk-takers,
pioneers and trail-blazers. Individuals with
courage and imagination who lived life as a daring adventure.
They called their discovery the NEW WORLD!
It was largely undiscovered before they came along.

Today we call our marketplace the NEW ECONOMY.
Or the new, new economy.
The latest version of our changing business landscape.
The common position for most companies and individuals
is something less than a daring adventure.
A far cry from discovery and learning.

Much of corporate America today has sadly become
inefficient operations. With high costs and a slowness to move
in these changing times. Big, slow, and outdated.
And somewhere within the organization, someone knows it
must change, but does not know how to accomplish the "update."

Take a look at your changing economic and life landscape.
What does it look like? What does it say to you?

PERCEPTION OR PERSPECTIVE

→

It's how we see things.
   Right or wrong, it's the information we use
to process how we feel or think about someone or something.

Sort of like the perception of SALESPEOPLE.
   The list usually goes something like this . . .
      pushy, obnoxious,
say anything, do anything,
                  less than truthful . . . Sound familiar?
That's perception.

When someone asks you how's business, and
      you answer based on circumstances like
the economy's slow, or the stock market's down, or it's Monday,
      or fine since it's Friday . . . that's you and your thinking
being affected by outside forces. It's your perspective of <u>things</u>.

And our Perspective *(Where we see things)*
can change our Perception. *(HOW we see things)*

Let's say you and I both leave the office at 5 p.m.
You start out driving your car on Independence Boulevard in
      Any City, USA, and soon find yourself in a four-lane
      traffic jam, making little or no forward progress.

Looking all around, forward and back, as far as you can see
      traffic is snarled. You may consider going back in the
direction you came, or finding an alternate route, or just becoming
frustrated right where you are.
You might hear yourself saying things like, "I knew it, I'll never get
to where I'm going now!" or "Just like EVERY OTHER TIME I
      try to get somewhere," or "Why am I even trying?"

At about the same time, I leave the office headed in the
same direction. The only difference is
I'm in a helicopter . . .
flying over the congested traffic.
And I can see that just a few hundred yards ahead of you
the traffic breaks and is flowing smoothly.

My perspective is different, and it is clear to me that you will arrive
at your destination on time and in a good frame of mind.
(Actually that second part's really up to you)

We both are seeing the same thing, but from a different perspective.
And what we see determines to a great degree,
our attitudes and confidence in reaching our goal
or objective. If I am now able to communicate with you what I see,
to encourage you that you will in fact make it,
will that now begin to affect your perception?
Of course.
Try improving your outlook on things before you
make decisions about how you *never should have gone
this route in the first place.*
There will be plenty of voices echoing
that advice if you attempt something daring
and adventurous.
Something uncommon and out of the ordinary.

Think how a helicopter pilot might see your situation,
how you might see it if you were above it, looking at it
objectively and not
"surrounded by the traffic" of negative thinking.

*"Not to go back is somewhat to advance;
a man must walk before
he can dance."*
—Alexander Pope

THINK LIKE A CHILD

What did you want to be
      when you were a child?
   When the world was shiny and new and full of possibilities.

   When you dared to believe that when those training wheels
came off, you'd still keep right on going.
Every day was like your own personal Discovery Channel.
     You'd go to bed at the end of the day with
       an expectation and anticipation for tomorrow and what
   adventures it would bring.

Where does that excitement go?

What happens to us over the years that conditions and programs us
to think like we're stuck on some chain-gang of daily drudgery?
     That every day's the same old, same old.

I've heard people make comments like,
"I've never had a job I liked."
"Work has never been something I've ever enjoyed."
                    How sad.
But not uncommon.
     There are many executives, workers, moms and dads who
   feel much the same way.

We should all reexamine the hows and whys that might lead us to
become stuck in a *"life rut"* feeling like "it can never change,"
     or "what's the use," or even worse,
"that can't happen for me, it's impossible."

"Always use the word impossible
with the greatest caution."
—Werner Von Braun

It's been said that solutions that cannot be discovered by a 40-year-old are obvious to a child.

I'm sure you've heard the story of the tractor-trailer truck that became lodged under a bridge. Stuck tight in the tunnel with lots of onlookers discussing how to raise the bridge or cut away some of the concrete; when an 8-year-old boy suggested, *"Why don't you just let the air out of the tires?"*

Just give it time, in 20 years or so we will have programmed that eight year old to forget the obvious.

We'll teach him or her to conform. To be normal. To be Average.

We'll test him to make sure he knows the "right answers," and how to think like everyone else so he can be "educated." Somewhere along the way he'll forget about those frivolous things like fun and discovery and adventure and learning and celebration and he'll be "one of us." That's why common exists, and uncommon is, well,

UN-common.

Daring to think that a thing is really possible even if it seems to be a daunting task, an enormous challenge.

That's the very thing that leads to discovery and achievement.

Doing the impossible.

Like Orville and Wilbur, or Tom Edison, or Walt Disney.

They didn't follow the crowd.

They wouldn't even listen to the crowd.

And one day, the crowd began to believe and followed them.

Dare to think big thoughts.

Ask yourself "what if?"

Challenge the status quo, don't let others shrink your dreams and big-picture thoughts and ideas.

GOLD
(or maybe just a 10% increase)

In his book *Business Beyond the Box* *(a great book I highly recommend)*
John O'Keefe relates a story about getting his shot at the
preliminary squad for Great Britain's Hockey team in 1972.

It was an eye-opening experience for him to see firsthand
how the team prepared for these games. He recounts
Britain's success as a hockey team in previous Olympics.
They finished 13th in Rome in 1960, 15th in Tokyo in '64,
and 14th in Mexico in '68.
So as Britain's hockey team prepared for the '72 games in Munich,
what do you suppose their goal was?

Some of the managers or supervisors I've had would do their
strategic planning and incremental improvement charts
and say to these young aspiring Olympians . . .
"OK, this year our goal is to get a 15% improvement
on our performance."
That sounds logical.

If our "average" finish is 14th
and we can somehow improve two positions to 12th,
then we've got our 15% increase and
an "all-time record" performance.

Is that what message you'd give to these young performers who
train for years, get up at 3 a.m. and run and skate and run
until they can't run and skate anymore?
Training for their shot at the Olympics so they can finish 12th?

The only goal . . . is Gold!

Forget the past, this is The Future,
and we will strive for the impossible!
To do something that has never been done . . . To make history!
That's what drives teams from underdogs to champions.

I can assure you that in Lake Placid in 1980,
    the USA team wasn't thinking
    "If we can just finish ahead of everyone else,
coming in second to Russia would be a good goal."
(Al Michaels described that memorable finish as "a miracle!")
Nope, GOLD!
Period.
Or better yet, exclamation point!

Put in the tape of your favorite *"underdog becomes champion"*
    or *"underdog makes history"* movie,
        and you'll immediately get the picture.
    Rocky, Rudy, Hoosiers, you choose. The message is the same.

So why is it that in today's marketplace so many organizations
    mortgage passion, inspiration, and high achievement
        for a 10% or 15% increase?
What we settle for in building and challenging ourselves,
or our teams, to strive for wouldn't produce the script needed
    for anything close to a *"we make history"* movie.

That's why they don't call it *"Mission: Do the Best You Can."*
Or *"Mission: 10% Improvement!"*
That's common.
Your mission is radical, dynamic improvement.
Mission Impossible! Do you accept?

Don't settle for common. Strive for gold.
Strive for history.
Do the impossible.
Become uncommon.

> *"Avoid the tranquilizing drug of*
> *gradualism."*
> —John O'Keefe, *Business Beyond the Box*

How Often Does Change Happen?

When I ask groups this question in a live session,
    they have the "right" answers.
"It's constant. It's always happening. Right now!"

Truth is, change is always happening AROUND YOU, but how often
is change happening in you?

How often are you changing how you think, how you learn,
    redefining what is possible?

If you think about it,
what was once impossible is now routine.
In lots of areas.
    What about light?
Once upon a time, the light bulb was a fantasy.
        That lunatic Tom Edison had already failed at something
like 999 experiments, and he certainly had no shortage of people
    around him delivering the *"I told you so"* seminar.
    The light bulb was IMPOSSIBLE!
But Edison didn't listen; he kept going and did the impossible.

How about flight?
The Wright Brothers didn't get it right the first time. Or the second.
    It seems that's what we're trying to teach our students
    and our workers today . . . "Get it right THE FIRST TIME!"
What kind of achievement lesson is that?
    History certainly doesn't support that lesson.
        How about this one:
        "Anything worth doing is worth doing well."
I take issue with that one too.

    Let's adopt the philosophy that says, **anything worth
        doing is worth doing POORLY,
<u>until you can do it well</u>.**

How do you suppose that might affect our achievement?

Now don't take too long to improve,
but keep at it if it's really worth doing.

I was just at Walt Disney World delivering a keynote address
to a national convention of association members.
(The message? Doing The Impossible!)
If you're ever there *(again)*, look around.
Hey they didn't get it all right the first time.
They kept at it because it was worth figuring out.
And so it is with many of history's
"impossible dreams." Consider this.

Something that you may right now feel is impossible,
will in fact, at some point in the future,
seem almost routine.
You may then say
you never had any doubts that this "impossible thing"
could happen.
Now ask yourself what impossible thing could happen for you?
And I don't mean winning the lottery.
I mean something you've always wanted to do, to be, to see . . .

And believe that it is possible.
Redefine what impossible really means.

Walt Disney once revealed his
secret to making dreams come true.
Wow, I got my pencil ready.
As a student, I wanted to know.

And since I have been to both Disneyland and Walt Disney World,
I know he has some credibility in this area.
He's made so many dreams come true he must have some
insight in this area, I reasoned.

His formula?

"Somehow I can't believe that there are
any heights that can't be scaled
by a man who knows
the secrets of making dreams come true.
This special secret—
curiosity, confidence, courage,
and constancy; and the greatest of all
is confidence.
When you believe in a thing,
believe in it all the way,
implicitly
and unquestionably."

The Walt Disney formula for making dreams come true.

There it is, from the mind of an uncommon individual who made history in the way he made *(and still makes)* dreams come to life.

4 things.

Curiosity, Confidence, Courage, and Constancy.

And to be confident in your pursuit of your dream.

Imagine being engaged on a daily basis
in making dreams come true.

Yours and others.

Give it a try and see how
this formula works
for you and your dreams.

Change.
Dreams.
Opportunity.

All are clues found on the way to radical improvement
    and dynamic results by countless students of success.
One of the great things about change is that
        change brings opportunity to you,
    or brings you to opportunity.

"We are changed."
—Denzel Washington,
in *Remember the Titans*

I love the movie *Remember the Titans*.
The line I'll never forget from that movie?
WE ARE CHANGED!
When Denzel Washington *(the actor who plays the coach)*
    stalks the practice field and announces to these young men:

*"We're gonna change the way we block!
Change the way we think. Change the way we WIN!*
We are changed."

Some things didn't change around them or were slow to change.
        Pride, prejudice, anger.
Frustration, ignorance, and "people's ways."
        Ever hear someone say,
"That's just not our way of doing things here."

Make change an inside job.
        Change the way you think.
Change . . . The way you learn. What you consider impossible.
    How you do things. So you can say,
"I AM CHANGED!"

My friend Bob works in career development.
That means, among other things, he helps individuals who
are in transition, experiencing change.

Maybe they're being laid off, or "sized" *(down-sized, right-sized, etc.)*
by their company. Bob helps them through the transition
process and to come out of that tunnel of change on the other side.

Going through a job transition is a tough thing.
I can speak from experience, having gone through a couple myself.

And it's not just a JOB transition, it affects
every area of your life. It affects those

around you. It's a life transition. A "life-changing" experience.
Bob works as a Senior Vice President with a company
called Lee Hecht Harrison.
Lee Hecht Harrison is a global career services company
with over 25-years experience in helping hundreds of thousands
of individuals move through a career transition.

Having the opportunity to work with them as a consultant
has given me new insight and a new appreciation for the
professionals there who counsel and assist others through something
that most all of us have experienced at one time or another.
Losing a job.

It's a time when you can have so many questions
running through your mind.
Often though, they may not be the right questions.
It's easy to lose focus in a transition and begin questioning your own
personal worth or value as a worker or manager in the marketplace.

That's where Bob and his associates come in.
With programs that help individuals refocus on the real
key questions that you should be asking.
Questions like:
What do I want to do? What do I need to do? Where do I start?

These programs include milestones to use as a guide
　　back to a productive position
with a new company or organization.

Their success stories are amazing. And one of the common
denominators from many of the individuals experiencing this type
of change is, *"This is the best thing that could have happened to me."*

Many of these individuals felt trapped or stuck in a rut or
　　dissatisfied with their jobs, but most say they would have
continued in the job had this downsizing or transition not occurred.

Working with Bob's company has given me
　　the opportunity to see up close the messages companies send
　　　　to their workers and managers.
　　　　Both to those individuals they ask to leave
　　and those they want to stay. Tough.

One of the areas where individuals going through this type of
　　transition can be affected most is in your personal value or

your perceived value
at that moment.

Our worth as an individual is so closely tied to our work,
our jobs, that in many cases when you lose your job for
　　whatever reason, you lose your sense of worth.

So the message to the individual is to work through the transition
process and the search process, finding another job or position.
　　And to understand that you still have value as a professional.
　　　　You are still a professional financial officer or a
　　professional human resources executive or a
　　　　professional whatever,
　　in the present tense.
And even though you don't have a job at the moment,
you still have worth and value. Both professionally and personally.

I mentioned earlier that I'll never forget the first time
I was introduced as

A Professional Speaker.

Wow.

It really had an impact on me.

Here I was doing something I loved doing, that I'd wanted to do
for a long time, and getting paid to do it.

A paid professional, earning my living doing this thing.

And as a professional speaker, you're paid to be good.

You should understand that even professional speakers sometimes
speak for free.

At lunches and banquets and civic groups.

When I speak for free, I still want to be good,

but now I can be *good for nothing!*

I sometimes use that story to get a laugh with audiences.

But that's exactly how it can feel when you're in transition,
like you're good for nothing.

Remember . . . you're still a professional,
you still have value, and someone's going to be fortunate
to find a talent like you.

How's that for a new perspective on losing your job?

I didn't say it was easy, but it's new.

It's uncommon.

Remember what we said at the beginning of the book?

It's worth repeating . . .

YOU ARE TALENT!

The marketplace wants to know about you.

How can you help them?

What's your talent?

What are you known for?

In business and economics we call that your brand.
Your image in the marketplace.
What are you doing to build your image,
to build your BRAND?

How has others' perception of you changed over the years?
Think about these companies and individuals.
How has their brand or the perception of them
changed over the years?

Cher
IBM
General Motors
O.J. Simpson
Microsoft
Paul Newman
Martha Stewart
Oprah
Enron
Times change.
So do brands and how they're thought of in the marketplace.

You've no doubt heard the term "reinventing yourself."
Changing the perception of what you're known for,
what your talent or value is.

> *"This time*
> *like all times is a very good one,*
> *if we but know*
> *what to do with it."*
>
> —Emerson

Branding is key to ad agencies, professional athletes,
     and almost every product and service.

Celebrities and movie stars were a great example of branding
     by the studios out in Hollywood years ago.

Recognize these names?
Norma Jean Mortenson.
Archibald Leach.
     Probably not as quickly as you'd recognize
          Marilyn Monroe or Cary Grant.
     That's why the Hollywood studios changed their "showbiz"
or brand names.
It was a part of the process of taking this brand of star
     to the public marketplace.

Getting the right name was part of the package.

Part of the BRANDING process.

Same for agents and agencies who must give their "product"
     the most memorable marketing message possible.

Remember these . . .
"Plop, plop, fizz, fizz . . ."
"Dirt can't hide from . . ."

"_____ tastes good like a cigarette should."
Get the idea? *(right, Alka Seltzer, Tide, & Winston)*

Go to work building your own personal brand. Your image at home
and in the marketplace. What are you really known for?

But . . .

What I hear occasionally from those attending my seminars is
how much they agree with all the things I've said . . . BUT.

(There's always a "but" lurking around somewhere, isn't there?)

And the "BUT" goes something like this . . .

*"BUT Michael,
what you don't understand is . . . as much as
I'd like to do all those things and read more and
do this or that,
I JUST DON'T HAVE THE TIME!"*

or

"I NEED MORE TIME!"

What to do?

Get ready.
I'm about to share one of Life's
greatest lessons with you
dear reader . . .

You Can't Manage Time

One of the greatest misconceptions in the workplace is
Time Management.

You're kidding yourself if that's your objective.
    At least you should redefine what you want to work on
    to be more productive.

Time is oblivious to anything you do or say.
It just keeps going. Regardless of what you do or don't do.
    It is beyond your ability to manage time.

A better goal would be to pay closer attention to how you
    use your time. And how you can be more productive in life
        and business within the time you have available to you.

Time to the MAX

I do have exciting news for you!
        Just so you'll know how very special you are . . .
YOU, that's what I said,
YOU are special.

And because you are, you have been given
    "The Maximum Amount of Time
        Allowed by Law!"

Sound silly?
I can assure you it's not meant to be.

It's meant to get you to take a look at what you wish for
    or the reasons you give for not doing something you know
you probably should be doing. It's what one teacher explains as the
difference between what's urgent and what's really important.

And no matter what you do, what your goal or objective is,
you can have no effect on time and how fast it travels.

Think about that for a second . . .

YOU have the exact same amount of time every day and
    every week as any person you view as special or exceptional
or successful or wealthy.
                    The same as the President and the Pope.
You have something in common with them all,
    something just like theirs.

Time.
    24 hours' worth in every day.
You can't get any more, as far as we know.
            Seven days a week. That's the most the law allows.

So let's see, 24 hours each day and 7 days in a week.
    That's 168 hours each and every week.
Same as Bill Gates. Same as Billy Graham.

And we know how they invested their time.

Powerful results
   ## are just as available to you.

It's not the time, it's the value you bring to it.
It's how you decide you'll use it. 168 hours a week for a lifetime.
            So how do you use it?
How will you use that time? That's the question you
    should be asking. Here lies a clue to becoming uncommon; what
you settle for in your choices, and where you spend or invest your time.

Let's say you need some sleep, and you do. SOME sleep.
Let's also say that as a starting point you establish 7.5 hours
            each night *(or day)* to recharge your mind and body.
It's optional of course, and some people push it.

Some need less, many take more than they need.
It's like they're making all these deposits into the
"sleep bank,"
hoping somehow that'll propel them to greatness.
Make them a better spouse or
parent or worker or leader. Wonder where they found that quote,
which book or tape or seminar is teaching this life lesson?

If, in fact, the gauge is 7.5 hours daily,
that's 52.5 hours of sleep each week.
That leaves at your disposal, to use however you choose,
115.5 HOURS EACH AND EVERY WEEK.
WHAT WILL YOU DO WITH THAT TIME?
How can you take the maximum amount of time
that the law allows you and create value
that returns incredible results in your life
and in whatever it is you choose to accomplish?

That's the challenge we all face for today and the future,
to get the most from what we've been given.
So it becomes not a question of TIME management,
but ME management.
"How will I choose to use my time?"
Ask yourself . . .
"Am I just spending it, or am I investing it?
Do I use my time for important things like
learning, improving, encouraging?
Am I giving any value outside of my
work environment to the really important things in life like
my spouse and kids, family and friends, recreation
and just a greater enjoyment of my life."

This is usually the place where some young corporate fast-tracker
fires back with "That's why I'm working so hard now,
so I can enjoy life later!" When exactly is later?
Is it circled on your calendar? When all your kids have grown up?

"Well if I'm gonna make it big, I've gotta put in the hours now!"
What's your definition of "making it big?" Getting rich?
Becoming wealthy and powerful?

If you only knew how special you are right now in the eyes of a child.

When I was five, eight, ten years old
I thought my Dad was the smartest,
strongest, most powerful and successful man on the planet.
Whether it was true or not, that was my perception at the time.
Take full advantage of that position while it's available.
When your son or daughter becomes 16 or 20,
that job has already been filled,
and you can't even get an interview. Make an impression
on your kids while they're still impressionable.
It's a great feeling and pays handsome dividends for life.

It really is sad, even tragic,
the low expectations you can have for the value of your
time, and the poor investments some make with that precious time.
The executive who pushes the envelope right to the edge
in his or her profession but neglects the value of family time,
or recreational time, or anything beyond that one dimension
of his or her professional life . . .
How can that be considered a success?

One thing you'll never hear from a father watching his son or
daughter leave home is . . .
*"Man, I'm sure glad I spent all that time at the office; wish I could
have jammed a few more hours a week into
staying late at work or being on the road."*

Hey, we all have to do what we have to do, but don't get a
martyr complex thinking *"I'm doing it all for you, honey!"*
That's not something your spouse and kids are buying,
so stop trying to sell it.

My kids have never once said,
*"Dad I sure wish you could have been away from home
more so we wouldn't have done all those things together."
"Gone all those places together . . ."*

Sound ridiculous?

So do the excuses I hear from people on why they don't perform
or add value outside of their work environment.

It also works with your parents.
Listen to the words of Harry Chapin's *Cat's in the Cradle.*
If you're a man who has any relationship at all with your dad,
it can't help but hit you right between the eyes.

The story of the song is about a busy dad and a little boy
who longs for just some time with his dad . . .

*"My son turned 10 just the other day, he said thanks for
the ball Dad, come on let's play,
Can you teach me to throw? I said not today—
I've got a lot to do, He said that's OK.
And he walked away, but he smiled every step and
said, 'I'm gonna be like him, yeah
you know I'm gonna be like him.'"*

The little boy grows up to be just as busy as his dad was.
And now it's the dad who yearns for time with his son. But
alas, the boy *"had grown up just like me, my boy was just like me."*

I think back to all the quality time I had with my dad when
I was a boy, and how I made it a point, even a goal
(that I'm happy to say I achieved),
to spend that same quality time with Ryan, my son,
while he was growing up.

But it seems no matter how much time we're
able to spend, it's never too much. It's never enough.

You could always use one more day
with your dad, or mom, or son,
or daughter, or spouse, or friend.

It's time you'll never look back on and say,
"Wish I hadn't done that."

"We all make mistakes in life.
It's what you do after the mistakes
that counts."
—Brandi Chastain
Soccer champion

THE MAN WHO SPLIT TIME IN HALF

As long as we're on the subject of time, just a word to the wise . . .
and those who aspire to be. If there were a man somewhere in
   the history of the world, who by His very existence in it,
divided time in half, wouldn't you, as a student, want to know,
   in fact, be driven to find out more about Him?

Even today, everyone uses the designation of time created
   by His coming into the world. Before Him one segment of time.
   And after Him, the other segment. Before Him and after Him!
Time broken up, split in two because of one Man.

Now that would have to be someone very important,
very significant, you'd have to say, to have the entire world
   as we know it to recognize a person who split time in half.

Surely you would say, *"That's someone I must find out more about."*
Well the good news is that of course, you can.

Not everyone has the story just right, so exercise caution
   in your studies, but there is a book, in fact a collection of books,
   that tell us much about Him.
      About His life and the value He gave to the time He had
      on this earth.
The New Testament recounts much of what is known about Him.
His name?

Jesus.

Jesus of Nazareth.
Jesus Christ.
Teacher, Prophet, Savior.

There are many titles given Him and regardless of what your opinion
is of Him right now, try to be open-minded in learning
about someone so special, so significant, so noteworthy
(there's a good word, worthy of taking notes)
that His arrival on the Earth divided time in half, B.C. and A.D.
Before Him and after Him.

But then some accounts say He is before all things and
after all things, Alpha and Omega. That sounds like
something we would have to look into. A mystery.

He is one Principal of time management
(maybe we should call it life management) that everyone
should learn more about.
You know He must have given some powerful seminars.

Great men are they
who see that the spiritual is stronger
than any material force.
—Ralph Waldo Emerson

CHANGE MANAGEMENT

This is in almost the same category as time management,
with an added wrinkle or two.

Change is coming, again.

Change is constant around you, though as we mentioned earlier,
not usually as constant within you. Someone once recounted
a conversation with a man who was celebrating
his 95th birthday.
*"Wow, 95 years. You've certainly seen
a lot of changes in your lifetime."*
"Yeah," the gentleman remarked, *"and I've been against 'em all!"*

Resistance to change is common.

And uncommon individuals like Edison, the Wrights, Bell,
Henry Ford, or Sam Walton can speed up the process in some areas.
But to expect that things will not change or to ignore
or resist change is to handicap yourself.

> *"That man who doesn't read
> has no advantage
> over the man who can't."*
> —Mark Twain

Riding Change

Horses are beautiful animals. Powerful and strong.
And able to increase our results and abilities as humans
when we can "harness" their resources.

Once upon a time we used them to pull plows and race and ride
for transportation or just for enjoyment.

But a young horse, full of himself,
does not care much for the idea of being ridden.
Especially for the first time.

You should try it some time, there's lots of snorting
and pawing and
resisting on the part of the animal.
And managing to get a rope
or bridle and then maybe a blanket and saddle on him is
just the foundation for this exercise in "change management."

I think you get the idea.
Once accustomed though, to rider and equipment,
the animal's value increases dramatically due to the change.
Riding "change" is a scary thing sometimes.
How'd you like to be the first astronaut strapped in on the nose
of a million pounds of thrust?
Knowing that at any moment, a jet-fueled inferno will
catapult you literally, out of this world?

Change is scary.
But without someone willing to say "I will,"
there would be only wild horses and
only unmanned space exploration.

Having the courage and the commitment
to ride the rocket of change can take you to places
of discovery and achievement that many individuals
could never have imagined.

And those common multitudes had
   no problem in sharing their opinions of those
  trying to throw a rope around the neck of change . . .
"It can't be done!" they'd say.
"It'll never happen." Or "I don't believe it."
Remember, in the beginning of change and new ideas,
the crowd is seldom right.

 Embracing and thriving on change is most certainly
uncommon.

Welcome change.
Prepare for it.
Keep up the learning curve so that change within us is as constant
 as the change around us.
   You can do it.

*"Change, Learning, and Leadership
are the Big 3 of the New Economy."*
         —*Fast Company* Magazine

What's the Difference Between
Learning and Training?

How about this?
A single event with a beginning and an end,

versus continuing improvement.

When you think about it, who controls training?
Someone else.
Your boss, your company, usually something or someone,
"out there."

Like the company who says,
"Yeah, we have training for all our new employees.
But we just finished it,
so it'll be another 6 months before we
do it again."

Oh, OK.
Guess I'll just wait here.
For Training.

Learning, on the other hand, is controlled by **you.**

The individual controls when, and how often, learning happens.
It's the desire to learn.
Wanting to get better, to learn something.
No matter when training will occur next.

Learning is an "inside" job.
You control it.
And it can continue for a lifetime.

When my son Ryan was six and just starting school,
I couldn't help being the interested and curious dad.

"What did you learn at school today son?"

I'd ask, leaning down to make eye contact
with this wide-eyed little boy. "Oh my gosh, Dad,"
he'd start excitedly, "We did this, and we learned about that . . ."
every day was something new and many of those new things
were of course things you and I might take for granted,
since we're not 6 years old
anymore.

This went on for awhile, each day with me asking what
he'd learned, and then a 6-year-old's excitement of his
daily discoveries being delivered to an interested adult.

One day after, "Hey son, what'd you learn today?"
He gave his learning list and then fixed those big brown
eyes directly on mine and quizzed me right back . . .

"Hey Dad,
what did YOU learn today?"

And then, as you might expect, I try doing the common
thing most anyone would do when we didn't do our home-
work . . . or that report at the office we're asked about . . .

"Uh . . . Well, son . . . See I'm the daddy, and . . ."
*(Ever notice there are times when you have what you consider legitimate
reasons for something you didn't do . . .
but in many of these cases every reason you can give
just sounds like an excuse?)*

What would you tell him?

That daddy's already know it all.

That daddy's are too old to learn . . . that you're a rocket scientist,
or you have 25 years of experience, or you're incapable of
learning anything new?

That you can't learn because you have a job now
and can't go to school?

Can't . . . can't . . . can't . . .

That was a challenge I never forgot.

A challenge from a six-year-old child to keep up the learning curve.

It's now something that excites me,
drives me, and is a major part of what I do . . . LEARNING!

"From my dad I learned never to give up.
He taught me it's better to go after
something special and risk starving
than to surrender."

—Jim Carrey, *comedian/movie star*

COURAGE

→

"Nothing noble was ever done without risk."
A picture with that caption hangs prominently over my desk in my office.

Do you ever consider doing something noble? Maybe historic? Consider the risk . . . and then go ahead, knowing that there will most certainly be a measure of risk involved.
So what?
Risk is everywhere.
I love the TV commercials that deliver a variety of situations that all end with the same message,
"Sometimes the greatest risk, is not taking one."

Risk

What is it?

As a young salesman I was once in the offices of Holiday Inn Hotels on the main corporate campus in Memphis, Tennessee.
While waiting for my meeting, I noticed a large frame hanging there with the following message . . .

"When Faced With a Choice
Between Security and Opportunity,
Always Choose Opportunity!"
—Conrad Hilton

I made a quick note of that one, since it seemed to have worked out pretty well for Mr. Hilton. That certainly speaks to taking risks, but it says little about gambling foolishly on one's future as seems to be the case with many individuals today.
Risk is necessary for discoveries and opportunities, but there is a certain amount of calculation involved in the process.

If you've ever heard Zig Ziglar's story, it can't help but inspire you
to be whatever it is you want to be. To take a chance, to go for it,
   whatever IT is for you.
It takes a bit of preparation for the journey though.

So read the books and listen to the tapes. As Zig often says,
   "You're what you are and where you are
      because of what's gone into your mind.
   You can change what you are and where you are,
         by changing what goes into your mind."

Even an ordinary person can start reading good books
      and listening to good messages and become extraordinary.
We know the right things to say it seems, and often many people
      talk and act like they want to be an oak tree.
But they live their life like they're in a flower pot.

It just doesn't add up. If you're going to be all you can be,
   an oak tree, you've got to get out of the flower pot
      and go where you can grow.
Cause out there where the real oak trees live, there's wind, rain
      and storms and animals climbing around on you . . .
It's risky, but that's how you grow.

And grow it does, that big oak tree just keeps on
      driving its roots deeper and reaching for the sky.
         If you really want to see "oak tree growth" in your life
and in our business, you're going to have to break some flower pots!

What can we do? What can you do?
Incredible things, unbelievable things.
   It's what we settle for that's the tragedy.

> *"Great deeds are usually wrought*
> *at great risks."*
> —Herodotus

Something must matter.

It's just as easy to embrace life and do whatever it is you do
with a fire, a passion.

Find your *"it."* That special something that paints a picture for
your imagination that includes passion, zest for life, zeal, resolve;
telling yourself you're going to keep trying . . . until.
Until you succeed.

That's the encouraging part of being a student.
Learning and investing what you've learned into
becoming more valuable, getting better.

I remember being at a seminar once with Les Brown.
Les is an enthusiastic guy with an obvious passion for
sharing his knowledge and life experiences.
"What you know has taken you to where you are," he said.
*"And what you don't know can take you where you want to be
and beyond."* That's true, but only if you
discover what you don't now know.
Believe in yourself and invest in your learning,
in your continuing education. Buy the books, get the tapes,
and get going on the road to getting better.

You deserve it!

DID YOU HEAR THAT?

Learn to listen . . . aggressively!

What does that mean? It means work at it. Listening makes up
such a large part of conversation. Communication.
It's been called an Art.

> *The real art of conversation is not so much*
> *saying the right thing at the right time.*
> *But also leaving unsaid the wrong thing . . .*
> *at the most tempting moment.*

Listening is communication.
Listening is understanding.
Listening is conversation,
and it is a large part of the art.

"A pair of good ears will drain dry a hundred tongues."

—Ben Franklin

Not listening aggressively or not really working at listening means
that most people think, *"I'm not talking, so I must be listening,"*
and that's just not true. Most of us listen like we're sitting at
a stop light. "Red, huummpff, . . . still red . . . almost, almost . . .
yep, it's green!" You're just waiting for that other guy to stop . . .
SO YOU CAN GO!
And the very moment you even think they're about to stop
talking . . . BANG!
Floor it, gotta get back to doing that thing you do so well,
talking! And in many cases you don't even wait for
the person to stop talking, you actually finish the sentence for them!

Know anybody like that? I'm guessing someone just popped
into your mind, and you're smiling right now.
Listen, really listen.

You just might learn something.

You'll also ensure that more often than not,
you'll understand the question. Is it that important?

A little boy returned home from his very first day at school
    to find his mother in the kitchen.

"Mom, where did I come from?"

he asked, looking up at mother.

Stunned, but unwilling to muster some falsehood about
storks or otherwise skirt the issue, the young woman knelt down
by her little boy and very slowly began to explain the facts of life.
    The youngster waited patiently, letting his mother stumble and
        stammer through a pained dissertation about men and
    women and babies and finally finished with,
"Do you understand now, son?"

"I don't think so, Mom.
I just wanted to know where I came from.
My new friend Billy came from Oklahoma."

Lesson in listening:
Make sure you understand the question.

Really Listen.

Did you know you can listen with your whole being?
Huh?

That's right, I said you can learn to listen with your whole being,
not just with your ears.
    Maybe I can explain it like this:
Did you ever say to someone, maybe a child, "Hey, listen to me."
        Only to have them say, "But I am listening."
And your response . . .
"Well, you don't *LOOK LIKE YOU'RE LISTENING!*"

That's right, you can look like you're listening.
How? By showing interest to the speaker. Try this.

Listen with your eyes . . . look at the speaker.
Listen with your body . . . lean forward.
Listen with your face . . . show facial expressions
    that convey your interest.
And lastly, listen with your voice.
Even a simple "hummm", or "oh,"
        or "wow" shows your interest and acknowledges
that you hear what the speaker is saying.

Sometimes you may not really hear what the customer,
            or your child or your spouse is saying.

Or you're not listening in an attempt to find a solution or
    solve the problem. I'm sure you, as I, have had
    any number of experiences where someone on the phone,
or behind a counter couldn't resist almost an impulse response, like
        "I'm sorry, we don't do that here,"
        or worse, when it almost comes out sounding like
"You must be stupid or something."
Like we have some nerve trying to be a customer.

"I am only one, but still I am one.
I cannot do everything,
        but I can do something;
    and because I cannot do everything,
I will not refuse to do the something that I can do."
—Edward Everett Hale

Have you ever found it difficult to be a customer?
You're ready to buy, if only someone would allow you to.

Case in point.
A man walks into a big-name video rental store
and says to the lady behind the register,

"I'd like to rent a blank video tape."

You might think that in this day and time, everyone's hip and with
it and knows how to hit the big numbers on Nintendo 64.

But the fact is, I can think of a couple of people who still don't use
the Internet or who might have a question about
something that you and I take for granted.

Predictably though, the lady behind the register quips back
to the older gentleman,

"WE DON'T RENT BLANK VIDEOTAPES."

The man tries again, *"Do you have blank videotapes?"*
"Of course we do," she says smirking now, "But we don't rent them.
Look mister, we rent videos for $3.95,
and we sell blank tapes for $2.95."
*"But I'll only be using it once, I only want to
rent the blank tape."*

Now I'll be the first to admit, that is not your everyday request.

But why is it often a first impulse to laugh or smirk or snicker and say,
"No, you can't be a customer today!"
Finally, the frustrated lady shakes her head and
goes behind a curtain.

A moment later a young lady who had overheard the exchange steps from behind the curtain with a smile, looks at the grandfatherly gentleman and declares, "Good day sir, we will be happy to rent you a blank video tape!"

The man's entire countenance changed as the young lady continued, "And we will rent it to you for only $2.95 plus tax."

"But the best part is you never have to bring it back. It's a lifetime rental!"

Sound silly?

It's our job to find a solution for the customer *(or any individual)*.

To solve the problem, make the "sale" with a smile, and all-in-all make the experience a pleasant one for that individual.

This young lady is obviously on her way to bigger and better things in her life and her career.

She is a student who's accomplished at giving value to the customer and will no doubt move on to greater challenges and greater achievements, largely because she knows how to really listen and help the interested party become a paying customer.

Sometimes it tough just trying to be a customer.

I mean you've got the money, you've made the decision, but that's still no guarantee you will actually be able to "buy" today. Sometimes you may need a little help.

The customer isn't always right . . .

But the customer is always the customer, as long as you'll allow him to be.

BE ENTERPRISING!

Ever been in a situation as a customer where you feel like
you're the good guy being tied to the train tracks by the bad guys
and you NEED HELP NOW! I mean the train is coming,
time is ticking, and someone comes up and wants to talk
about the ropes, or the tracks, or the train,
when what you really need is rescuing.

Here's one of my "train track" experiences.
I love Enterprise Rent-a-Car. I love that they pick me up.
I love that they know me at my local branch and make me
feel special *(even though they pick everybody up)*, but mostly I love it
because Andy, Jennifer, and Matt and the rest of their team
have the kind of mentality that I'm about to relate to you,
an uncommon attitude about serving the customer. ME! And
making me feel like I, and my business, matter to them.

They even offered to make my reservations *in other markets
where I travel to speak!* I didn't ask them to do that,
but they came to know my business and one day Jennifer,
the branch manager, offered to make a reservation for me
at an Enterprise office halfway across the country . . . wow,
just another reason to love doing business with
my personal car rental division . . . which is how they make me feel.

This kind of service is certainly uncommon and
can sometimes cause a glitch here and there for other branches
around the country who may not encounter this special kind
of service on a regular basis.

Recently I had planned on making a trip to Dallas with
The Woman *(My Wife Sandi, I'll explain later,)* and Lindsay.
At the last minute I delayed my trip, but the
girls went on down and attempted to pick up the
rental car at DFW Airport's Enterprise counter.
So, Sandi's in Dallas, and I'm in Charlotte.

My local office had made the reservation, and there was a mix-up
about the deposit *(I almost never pay a deposit)* and Sandi realizes
    she doesn't have a credit card with her to cover the
$250 deposit, plus the rental fees. So I try to pay over the phone
            (can't do it . . . for my own protection, which I understand),
    I offer to fax in a copy of the front and back of card
        with my signature *(which I have done for hotels in a couple of instances),*
            but again the answer is the same.

As I take the time to explain the situation on the phone,
    Sandi's there in Dallas, waiting at the counter for her car.
I'm a long-time, loyal Enterprise customer
            in Charlotte, trying to "buy" but making little progress.
Meanwhile back at the airport in Dallas, after hearing my story,
    Juan does two things, both of which take
my level of frustration up a notch.

Number 1. He apologizes.

Next time you're in the middle of a crisis, say an oncoming train . . .
try apologizing and see where it gets you.
        There is certainly a time and place for an apology,
    but this is not one of them.

Number 2. Juan quotes me *"our policy."*

Try the oncoming train test with this one too. I'm not interested
in Juan's apology, and I've done business with Enterprise for years,
    so I know as much about their policy as I care to.
        Two strikes. And I'm feeling low and outside.

I persist though, asking Juan . . .
    "What are our options? What can we do?"
I ask *"What if this?"*
Nope.
"What about . . . ?"
Can't do it.

Finally a glimmer of hope that I could still be a customer today . . .
    Juan says,
*"Well, I suppose if you could get your local branch to be responsible for
the charges . . . we could maybe bill them . . . "*
AHA!
    I tell Juan someone will call him back, me or the local branch.

My next call is to my local Charlotte Enterprise office, remember
it's Saturday morning and I have one hour before they close.
    Jay answers the phone. I relate my story, as briefly as possible,
telling Jay what Juan has told me, and without hesitation,
Jay begins to respond as though he's on a movie set and the director
        just yelled action . . .

"Where are you now?" Jay asks.

I'm in Monroe, 25 minutes away . . .
"Let's do this . . ." Jay says thinking out loud,
    *"You go by and see Chad in our Monroe branch,
        tell him I'll fill him in later, let him make an imprint
        of your credit card and I'll call Juan in Dallas."*
I'm almost speechless, and then Jay says the magic words of
UNCOMMON . . .

"Don't worry Mr. York, I'll Make It Happen!"
I almost yell back into the phone . . .
*"Now that's what I wanted to hear Jay . . . make it happen!
    You are the man!"*
Jay laughs, and in less than 15 minutes, Sandi is driving her
Enterprise rental car to the hotel in Dallas.
    I am still in Charlotte, where Jay has made me once more
a happy customer. Did I mention I love Enterprise?

How do you respond when your customer is on the
train tracks looking at that oncoming train?
In a time-sensitive crisis situation,
and desperately wanting to be a paying customer?
Try the Jay response . . . *"I'll Make It Happen!"*
Someone is sure to go away smiling.

"Faced with a choice between
changing one's mind
and proving that there is no need to do so,
almost everyone gets busy
on finding the proof."
—John Kenneth Galbraith

Define CUSTOMER

If I asked you to give me your definition of customer, could you?
When I ask that question to live audiences, it's interesting
to hear the kind of responses I get.
At first it might seem to be an easy one until you try to
define or describe it. It's almost taken for granted to mean
someone who buys from you or someone who exchanges money
for goods and services. Without making lots of lists,
and having different lists and definitions,
let me give you another way to think about customers.

My definition of customer?

The object of your communication.

Think about that.
    You have "customers" that "buy" from you every day,
    but they may never spend money when they do it.

Is your spouse a customer?
        You better believe it.
Your child? Sure.
You have lots of customers you come in contact with every day.
At work, at home, in clubs and organizations; any number of people
    and groups who are weighing the "product" of YOU every day.

Uncommon companies know they have lots of customers
    inside the organization, as well as outside.

An Organization on the brink . . .
It's 1978.
An organization sits on the brink of disaster.
The common perception is that the company will be bankrupt
    in a matter of months, maybe weeks.

The battle is waged on many fronts.
  From "customers" who have purchased their products
to prospective buyers who are buying from the competition instead.
Workers fear shutdowns and layoffs; the rumors fly.
      Public opinion certainly doesn't favor the organization,
        and rumors fuel the fires of impending doom.

Dealers who sell new products from the factory and the resellers
    of used products are understandably fearful and cautious.
          And the big picture includes, and affects,
          the economy and even lawmakers.

The company is Chrysler.

Enter Lee Iacocca.
One of the greatest "selling" jobs in economic and automotive history.
What happened?
He turned things upside down.

He went to the moon and took Chrysler with him.

He SOLD his vision and ideas to the workers and the buyers,
        found favor with the general public,
            instilled confidence in his dealers,
    attracted top industry talent, and along the way convinced Congress
        to provide Chrysler with the largest federal loan in history
at that time . . . and on top of all that, proceeded to pay it back well
ahead of schedule.

Who was his customer?

Everybody.

Or anybody who was the object of his communication.

Customers inside and outside the organization.
And you have them too. You have supervisors or workers
in other departments that can take you closer to or farther from
    your objectives based on how they feel about you,
        and how they respond to you.

Remember . . .

You're more powerful as a communicator when you
understand first.

So go to work making a positive impact on
all the customers around you.

History says, people will notice.

"Everyone needs recognition for his
accomplishments, but few people make the
need known quite as clearly as the little boy
who said to his father,
'Let's play darts. I'll throw, and you say
Wonderful!' "

—from *Bits & Pieces*

WORDMANSHIP:
THE POWER OF WORDS!

Once we listen and understand, then comes our opportunity
   to speak. To use the power of words.

This is one of my favorite things to learn and teach.

Words are powerful!
If the pen is mightier than the sword, the spoken word
         is a dramatically more powerful tool *(or weapon)*
      that can be used for good or evil.
To build up, or to scar and destroy.

Never forget that words once spoken can never be retrieved.
      You can write a letter and not mail it, have a change of heart,
         throw it away, and everything is fine. But a careless word spoken
in anger or ignorance . . . hear me now . . . ***can never be undone!***

You may ask for forgiveness and even receive it, but the pain,
      the memory of that moment,
                  how it made someone feel . . . is a lasting impression.

The writer of an ancient Hebrew script says that some words are
Alive! Active! Full of Power,
         and sharper than a doubled-edged sword.
         Wouldn't you like to know which word
or words the writer's talking about? Good News! You can.

If you're really committed to being a student, it's out there
for you to find. A wise man once told me if I wanted things
      to be different for me, I had to be different.

At first I didn't understand,
         but I went looking for clues and there it was.

He meant I couldn't get better, things couldn't get better,
until I expanded my knowledge, increased my value,
   asked better questions, and invested what I learned.
In essence, he summed it all up in this phrase;
   "If you continue to think like you've always thought,
      you'll continue to get what you've always got."
Wow, that was deep. But simple enough for even me to understand
   at the time. Let me give you an example on the use of words.

For years I studied and wrote and worked at expanding my use
of our language, learning to communicate, building my vocabulary.
On more than one occasion, someone would make the comment,
   " You're really a **Wordsmith**!"
      And of course they meant this as a compliment
to my speaking style and use of words.

IF I HAD A HAMMER . . .

If you've ever heard the term "Wordsmith"
where do you suppose it gets its beginning?
   How about the root "smith"?

What was a smith? . . . Hummmm.
Remember the verse that goes,
"Under the spreading chestnut tree, the village smithy stands . . ."

That's right a smith, or smithy, was actually a **Blacksmith**.
And what did he do?

He worked with black iron, and pounded that iron with a giant
hammer to form it into the shapes of tools he, and others, needed.
   He was great with black iron and hammered it into submission.

So after taking a closer look, would you compliment someone's
use of the language by saying they really knew how to take a
   hammer and bang around on those words?
      Oops, not exactly what I meant . . .

Now let me give you another mental picture of what
I'd like to encourage you to become,
only if you're interested in being one of the best
at whatever it is you do.
Think about this word . . .

Swordsmanship

Swordsmanship!

So what image do you get when I say "swordsmanship?"
How about a musketeer *(not mouse-keteer)*
you know a musketeer, as in "The Three . . ."
or better yet, Zorro!
Yeah, Zorro.
That's it!

Deftly handling his blade, a master swordsman, defender of good.
Is there anything about that image that makes you think
he could be good with a hammer?

Or can you picture a Blacksmith, dropping his apron and hammer,
grabbing a saber, and giving Zorro a lesson he'll never forget?
I don't think so.
Their skills and approaches are worlds apart.
So let me give you a new word . . . ready?

Wordsmanship.
There it is, Wordsmanship!

Deftly handling words with all the skill and finesse of Zorro
with his blade. My challenge to you is to become a Wordsman
*(Yes ladies, you too, it's still called wordsman,
cause **wordswomanship** loses something in the translation.).*

So whenever I take the platform to speak,
    or enter a meeting with a
        co-worker . . .
AHA! En garde!
I, Michael York, student and CEO . . .
    prepared to instruct and inspire
with the deft handling of wordsmanship!

Now if you've ever seen any of the Zorro shows through the years,
    you know that those bumbling sergeants have swords too.

But it's not the same.
Having the skill, and having the potential of the weapon
without the skill are different.
        Remember, the blacksmith can have a sword too,
    but that doesn't make him a match for our hero.
Touché.

*"We know what we are,
but know not what we may be."*
—Shakespeare

THE ART OF PERSUASION

Persuasion.
Wow, there's a great word.

The skill or ability to persuade. It's an art.
And while some people create art with brushes, we've already established that some use hammers. They lack the skill of a brush, but anyone can hit something with a hammer *(see wordsmith)*.

We use persuasion,
or at least have the opportunity to use it every day.
Everyone sells something.

Children are masters of persuasion.
They start even as newborns by screaming at the top of their lungs, and even as new parents we respond.
We are *"persuaded"* to pick them up, change them, feed them;
we just keep looking for the result the child is attempting to persuade us toward.

We're motivated!
Because we want them to have whatever it is they need.
And we want the screaming persuasion to stop.

Husbands and wives certainly practice the art of persuasion on one another. And that's how it should be.
I'm reminded of a story I heard about a man who was offered a promotion by his company.
He was very excited about the new position,
but it would require him relocating to North Dakota.

When asked if his wife would relocate, he said,
"Oh, she'd relocate, but not to North Dakota!"
When he was asked what he actually knew about North Dakota, he replied honestly "Nothing."

Asked what his wife knew about North Dakota,
    again his response,
"Not anything." His boss then questioned why he thought
    she wouldn't move there,
        to which he replied, "Would you?"
Get a mental picture of this situation.
This man, in his ignorance of North Dakota *(the product)*

is about to persuade his wife
to NOT DO
something he wanted her to do.

It's done every day in life, and in the profession of selling.
He'd probably start her out with some classic opening remark like,

"You wouldn't want to move to North Dakota,
would you?"

And then she would give him "The Look"*(every man has seen it)*,
and say, "Goodness NO!" She would being doing in fact,
    exactly what he was persuading her to do given his attitude,
        raised eyebrows, questioning tone, and all the other signs
    that gave the nonverbal signals of
"Yeah, that's exactly what I thought you'd say."

So his boss, obviously an accomplished student of persuasion
and the magnificent game of skill, PERSUADED his newly
        promoted supervisor to present the "opportunity" to her
            in the following manner.

"Honey, how would you like it if I got a BIG promotion
and we moved to **A PLACE LIKE** Denver?"

 "Denver has lots of great qualities, lots of football fans, lots of
outdoor enthusiasts, fresh air, mountains with great skiing,
        and terrific quality of life."
Then when his wife gave an indication that said,
"Sure I'd consider that," he would continue with
        his positive persuasion.

"It's actually a place that's BETTER THAN DENVER . . .
IT'S NORTH DAKOTA!"
(Don't stop now and wait for a response, continue with the art...Now for the climax.)
"It's the way Denver used to be before so many people started
moving there, and it has skiing, great schools, an unspoiled
quality of life with clean mountain air and water . . ."

Get the picture?

I don't know if he ever took that promotion and relocated
    to North Dakota's pristine and unspoiled beauty,
but I do know that any proposal can benefit from an honest
        presentation of the best qualities and characteristics
        extended for consideration.
Did you get all that?
I sure didn't ask the woman I wanted to be my bride,

"Honey,
        If you don't get any better offers,
would you consider marrying me?"

And I also didn't launch into a laundry list
    of my less-than-desirable attributes, like,

"Sweetheart, I know I'm just getting out of the military,
and I don't have a job, and I don't have any money saved up,
        and I don't have a house,
            or really any idea where we might live,
    but if you'll have me . . ."
                        # You must be kidding!

It wouldn't take a rocket scientist to hear all that and say, **"Next."**
    Just remember, half the fun of getting presents is the
attraction to the wrapping of the gift.

MUSIC

⟶

If we can all agree on the power of words, then there should be little debate that their power increases with a little music mixed in. Don't neglect good music as something to add value to your life.
And I guess the only caveat here is,
be careful how you define "good."

Music can do incredible things.

It can move you, excite you, calm you, inspire you, or stir you. How can you hear the *Star-Spangled Banner* and not feel more patriotic? I can't believe any American could watch the tape of Whitney Houston singing the National Anthem at the Super Bowl during Desert Storm, with the jets flying overhead and the flag flying in the breeze, and not be moved.
Not be proud to be an American.

The land of the free, the home of the brave.
Hey that's where we live, you and me. Put some horns and drums and cymbals in there and wow, it moves your emotions. That's what music is designed to do, to move you, emotionally.

There are lots of songs and lots of types of music.

Songs that pick you up, songs that make you cry,
songs that tell stories, and songs that don't really make sense but just make you feel good.
There's country and pop and rock and jazz and all sorts of labels we put on our music. Some we call "bubble-gum" and some gives us the "blues."

Some of the most moving, most powerful music has come to us through the movies.
Hey wonder how they came up with that word . . . MOVIES.

Most movies do move us.

They move you along as they paint a picture, tell a story, shock you,
      inspire you, make you laugh. They move you.
   And I can't remember many, if any, that didn't use music
to help in the movement. I'm sure you can think of some great
music, great songs, that you first heard in the movie theater.
      We called those "musicals," movies and plays in which music
         was an integral part of the production.

One of the greatest, according to the test of time, may have been
The Sound of Music. The saying goes that music has the power
   to "soothe the savage beast." Music can convey
   powerful messages, sometimes you're not even aware of.
   Hey, they don't make movies anymore without music;
they call the music that moves the movie along *"the score."*
The musical score.
         It's hard to imagine a movie without music.

I know if you like music at all, there are songs you can remember
      the words to that you first heard years,
         maybe even years and years, ago.
         One example is something most any of you who
         wake up to a clock radio have experienced.

When that music comes on at the designated time,
      you may only hear a few moments of a song that's playing.
But whether you hit the snooze button or get on up and
         head for the shower, almost magically something happens.

Your incredible thinking
machine, your mental computer, grabs that few moments
of a song and fills in the blanks. I mean if it's a song you know,
      it seems you're humming or singing it or just hearing it
         in your mind. Wow, how powerful is that?

And the good news is it works the same way with good messages,
stories, sermons, or cassettes that you hear over and over,
they get in there. For good. To stay.

They become a part of you.

Having said that, *beware of the other stuff.*
Messages that you don't need in there.
Messages or music.
A great melody that soothes or stirs can do long-term damage
in that intricate computer that is the mind, the soul;
if the lyrics to that music aren't the kinds of words you'd
use to tell a story to your mother or your children.

Be on guard, for there are some out there who get
a twisted enjoyment out of wreaking havoc on your life.
Now and in times to come. Find that one hard to believe?

You don't have to look much further than recent outbreaks of
computer viruses to understand this one. These viruses are sent
into personal and corporate systems like a stealth bomber
on a mission to destroy. Talented minds that use
their intellect and knowledge not for good, to build up;
but to tear down, erode, stall, impede, or even destroy.
Then laugh about it. It's sad. But it's true.

Giant computer systems or websites that are paralyzed by some
email waiting to explode or some toy-soldier program
that makes thousands and thousands of personal computers
call one site all at the exact same time. Bringing about
at least a temporary, if not more permanent, breakdown.

So without me going much further down this road,
understand that there are those whose goal,
whose very existence is to cause destruction.
And to develop destructive devices. I don't know why,
I just know that as a student you cannot ignore it.

When I talk about music, I have a pretty good background
    to draw from. One of my earliest jobs, my fourth actually
*(working in our family business at age 12, supermarket stock clerk, and sportswriter
for our local paper)*, was in radio.

I started working at a small local station at age 15, WDXE.
That was a blast. Imagine being in high school and being a
    disc jockey at the same time. I loved it.
            And for a long time I thought
that's what I wanted to do, be on the radio, or in radio, as my career.
    That eventually changed, but what never changed
            was my love for music.
What did change was how I heard many of the words
of those songs,
then and now.

What's also changed, and not for the better, are the
            words *(I think those are words)* in some of the music today.
    And it's not just the getting older, out-of-touch thing.

Hey, I know I'm older, but music has become like much of the
    rest of our culture today, fragmented and segmented and
all over the board. And in some cases, it can hardly be seen as
being for the better . . . much of our music and lyrics today
        have become a sort of computer virus.

Even the names of groups and messages on the covers of CDs and
tapes are sending poisoned arrows aimed at a specific target . . .

You!

And your mind. Your inner being.
It's not unlike some Trojan horse that's just looking for an opening
to cause decay and destruction. Especially with young people.
    If we agree on the power of words, we must be smart
enough to know that it works for good and for bad as well.

So keep your guard up.

Remember, changes happen to you when you begin to change
what goes into your mind. Often it can be subtle changes,
especially in the beginning. You may not even notice, but those
around you will. What are you programming into your memory?
You get to decide.

You choose, for good or bad.

Don't allow just anything in the "living room" of your
mind. Look through the little "peep hole" in the door, before
you let just anything in there.

My advice? Be on guard.

Especially to my young friends, pre-teens and teenagers, I know
what it is to love music. To have it play such a big part of the love
and zest and emotion in your life.

But be sure to make a careful evaluation of

what you're becoming in the company

of your music and lyrics. And in the company of your
friends who listen to them.

If someone you dearly loved could understand the words,
would you be embarrassed?

How would you feel? And if you say

"I wouldn't feel anything . . ." *(I've heard that answer before)*
it only proves that the Trojan horse has already begun the invasion.

How about you look for more of the good, the clean, the pure, the
powerful, and the positive? That's the goal.
More good stuff going into your "personal" computers.

And what about the people you spend time with?

Could they have any effect on you?

Our legal system has some pretty strong opinions on this one.
Even if you're not the individual committing the act,
but you're there with someone who is, it's evidence of
your actions and intentions.
Assisting, aiding, and abetting.

It's known as being "guilty by association."

THE POWER OF
ASSOCIATION

John Maxwell is one of my favorite writers. His books on
leadership provide some great ideas and instruction
    for most anyone, from executives to parents.

His lessons on the power of association are simple and powerful.
Consider.

1. Where you go determines who you meet.

It's true.

If you find yourself on the wrong side of town at 3 a.m., you
already know who's *(the type of individual)* going to be there.
    Suppose you'd find some community leader,
        or get some good instruction from a successful businessperson
    or maybe run into your mother?

You already know pretty much who's waiting for you there,
        and so do I. Ask an officer of the law
    what they think about this one.

2. Who you meet determines how you think.

Do you realize that the people you associate with, the individuals
you meet and spend time with are shaping how you think?

What and how you think about life, authority, music,
        politics, parents, whatever. I've witnessed this firsthand,
        and if you consider it for just a moment, you have also.

It's one of the reasons I say you can't change people.

You and I can't get them to do something they don't really have
        any interest in doing. But if you or I can change how they
think, change their minds, then they begin to change themselves.

Same as before, for good or bad. It's a powerful principle.

Ask a parent their thoughts on this one. And why parents care
who their child is hanging around with or dating or friends with?

What do you think? And who's influencing your thoughts?

3. How you think determines what you do.

How you think or feel about something will shape your attitudes
   toward it. What you believe is possible, or impossible.
   If you worked around people like Disney's Imagineers,
who come up with incredible ideas and make the extraordinary
seem almost routine, Would it affect you and how you'd
do your job? Or what you choose to do as your life's work?

How you think has everything to do with the paths you take and
   the choices you make in life. Because that's how we're made.
   We get to choose. Choose to hang out and underachieve, or
      choose to go to the moon.
   Whether you take responsibility for how things work out or go
to work building a list of who and what to blame.

4. What you do (every day) determines what you become.

This is the culmination of all of the above. How association
works for you or against you. How the law of inertia works
for you or against you. Whether you have momentum on your side
   or you've chosen to give momentum away,
         in your life or in your career.

John Maxwell is a genius.

Or at the very least a good student who paid attention and took good
notes. What could you learn about life and leadership from him?
It's fundamental instruction we can all understand.

   It's something we've all witnessed it at one time or another.
And it's TRUTH.

If you and I begin spending major time together,
   only one of two things can happen.
You will become more like me,
      or I will become more like you. That's it.
And if it sounds oversimplified, consider the lessons of history.

Read some biographical accounts of historic individuals
   who changed the landscape of our country, our society.
   Do your part as a student and you will find the answer
      that you already know is true.
      A model or a mentor or a manager who impacted
      people by his or her association with them; a dynamic
   and historic story of success, or failure, by association.

Take some time to reflect on where you are in your life
      and how the power of association has worked
         for you or against you.
And know that wherever you are in your life, it still works.

I hear individuals talk about what's happened to them or about
traumatic events in their lives or their childhood
   and how, *"that's why I'm the way I am today."* Sad.

But understand this.
While you can't go back and change the beginning,
you can absolutely begin today and change the ending!
   You have the power to change how it all works out for you
in the end. To write the ending of your story
   the way you want it to work out.

To make the last chapters of your book and your life
                     the best ones.

And the power of association is one of the major keys.
   It's one of the power tools that you have available to you.

If you know you're spending too much time with the wrong crowd, change it. That single decision will bring about dramatic changes in your life and work.

It can change your mind and begin to change many things about you.

I've spoken to numerous organizations and trade associations and groups on this very thing.

The real power of association is people.

People who can do incredible things when they're challenged or called upon to do them.

It's the things we can do together that none of us can do alone.

That's teamwork.

That's The Power of Association.

"Momentum is the greatest of all change agents."

—John Maxwell

SONS AND DAUGHTERS, MOMS AND DADS:
(You can learn a lot from your family.) →

I love kids!

I love how they look at life, how they learn
and how they ask questions. Maybe not deep,
thought-provoking questions in the beginning,
but they keep asking till they get an answer.
Sometimes even after they get the answer,
if it's not the one they're looking for.

Think back about how you as a six-year-old looked at life
and learning.

Children at a young age are so impressionable.
Every day is brand-new. They have very little to compare it to,
they don't rely on "experience," they're open to new things,
new ways of doing things they already know about, new ideas.

Learning is everywhere,

a constant companion. It is an amazing world for a six year old.

When do we lose that amazement of learning along the way?

My wife and I have two beautiful children that are
the joy of our lives. We also have a host of nieces and nephews,
and it sometimes seems like people just drop by
to let us use their kids for a while *(only kidding)*.

And while kids need instruction, and they can be good students,
they can also teach US a lot.

For one, they have no problem conveying their expectations on exactly what it is they want.

I have some audio cassette tapes of Saturday afternoons
when my son and daughter were very young.

With Lindsay in her high chair, *(she couldn't be more than 2)*
the conversation goes something like this . . .

Me: "Are you hungry?"

Linz':   "O'nt kake" *(Translation, Could I have cake please?)*

Me: "You need to eat lunch first, how about some beans?"

Her: "O'NT KAKE!"

Me: "No, lunch first. What about a hot dog?"

Her: "No! Kake!"

Me: "NO KAKE . . . I mean, cake."

Her: *(with increasingly bigger drooling smile for effect)*
          "'O'nt kake, bay-buh" *(baby)*.

Me: "No, cake bay-buh, hot dog?"

Persistent child: "O'nt kake, bay-buh . . ."
            "Love you too, Daaa-Deee!"
Me: "*(Folding like a card table)* Here's your cake, sweetheart . . ."

Take a lesson from a child near you; learn to convey your
expectations and have some heart. Be persistent.
I remember hearing a friend say once we should learn to
     sell like a child and take rejection
              like a puppy.

The room exploded in laughter,
     because everyone can relate to those two illustrations.

If a child asks, and you say no, do they ever ask again . . . Puulleeze . . .

A child is nothing if not committed and persistent.

They keep on asking.

And how about that pup, when you come home in the evening to the li'l mongrel *(that you didn't want, but your kid just kept asking for),*

You plop down in your chair and the little furball is all over you.
Ears flopping, tongue licking, and tail wagging . . .
so you swat him once with the newspaper.

That might deter him for the moment but just a look in his direction and Bang!
He's back, new and improved, stronger than ever.

A puppy doesn't know what rejection is. He just wants to be the object of your affection and recognition.

Not a bad lesson for us to learn from kids and dogs.

CHOOSE YOUR WORDS

→

Whether you're communicating with a prospect, long-time
customer, your spouse, a child, or your mother, you should practice
    using key words. Choose them carefully.
Probe! If "how" you say it is important, and it is,
        what you say, the words you choose, are key to
    communicating your message.

Anytime you're engaged *(good word, and not just for marriage)*
        with someone in a conversation or presentation,
            you're conveying information with an expectation.

You can learn some valuable lessons in this area
    by becoming a parent.

It's just a by-product of parenting, though I wouldn't recommend
        becoming a parent just to learn this lesson . . .
    you can ask someone who is a parent as an option.

My daughter Lindsay is the love of my life.

So is my wife, my son, and . . .
    you get the idea.

But there is something special between a father and a daughter.
        If you're either one, a father or a daughter,
            I'll bet you can't listen to
Bob Carlisle's song *Butterfly Kisses* without tearing up.
        You can feel that song on the inside. It's just special.
            And if you don't believe kids can sell . . . ask a parent.

Kids sell with logic, and they sell with emotion.

And when I say they "sell," I mean they convey information
    with a goal or an expectation in mind.

> *"Ask and it shall be given you;*
> *seek and ye shall find;*
> *knock and it shall be opened unto you."*
>
> —Matthew 7:7

When Lindsay was younger, she absolutely couldn't go to bed at
                night without being tucked in. She had this
            stuffed dog she named *"Longbody"*
                (for obvious reasons, it was, well, you know . . .),
so every night it's Longbody, Lindsay, and me tucking into bed.

And for many years that meant reading a *"bed-nite"* story.
        I remember some nights thinking, or even saying,
                    "Why don't you just go on to bed sweetheart,
I'll tuck you in tomorrow night . . ."

"No," she'd say, **"Tonight!"**
And so off we went for the "bed-nite" session.

Now I'd pay to be able to do that again.

That was treasure.
And sometimes you're right there, in the middle of the treasure,
        and you don't recognize it until you and all those
                treasured moments have moved on.

I'm so thankful for all,
and I do mean every single night that I was a part of
        those "bed-nite," tucking-in sessions.

That girl can sell.
And I'm so glad I said yes to all those little sales presentations
        while I still had the chance to buy.

She'd draw and write things that most children draw and write,
and fortunately her mother and I saved many of them.
   I take them out from time to time and laugh a little,
         cry a little, and remember when.
   During many of those times it seems we didn't have
much else than each other, but it was treasure nonetheless.

I've often used Lindsay in conveying to my students and audiences
over the past 10 years the difference between
      "logic," and "emotion."

Most sales people sell with logic, or try to.

That's what accountants sell with, logic.
      Numbers make sense; they're logical.
   What you don't find much of are accountants that use emotion
to get their point across to the CEO, or to whomever it is
      they're presenting information.

Unfortunately, many aspiring sales professionals also neglect
      the power of emotion in their presentations.

Let me give you an example.

My little girl *(she's now 19)* has, most every year,
            given me a card for my birthday or Father's Day
      or other special occasions, and she signs it with something like,
"Love" or "With Love," or "Love you, Dad . . ."
            you get the idea.

Now that's sweet and touching, but after all she is my daughter
and I am her dad and she loves me and has no problem writing that
      in the card. It makes sense. It's logic.
   It's logical that a daughter should love her dad.
And that does get a result or response when I read it.

But when she would climb into my lap and drape her arms
around my neck and look into my eyes and smile . . .
then lean over and whisper in my ear,

"I love you Daddy."

BANG, DID YOU FEEL THAT?

I'm not asking if you read it, I'm asking if you felt it?
That, my friends, is emotion.
Message delivered, message received.
And I melt like Frosty the Snowman in Yuma, Arizona.
I'm Jello. Putty in her hands.

Her mom has this little gesture she does whenever Lindsay is
asking for something. She just holds up her hand and makes a fist
with her little finger sticking out.
Oh brother.
You know, like she's telling me that there I am wrapped
around her daughter's little finger . . . and she's right.

I still have to be the Leader, the Parent,
but if I can give my daughter value and make her happy,
well that sounds like a worthy ambition to me.

Remember, the eye is logic, and the ear is emotion.
And the response to each is
very different.

It takes both to make an effective transfer of information
toward the end results you seek.

So when you're involved with others, show a little passion.
Sometimes a little emotion can be a great thing.

Look up the word "rejoice" in Webster's dictionary.

I could tell you what it means, but it'll do more for you
if you look it up on your own.
Now, guess how many of you reading this will actually look it up?
Answer, 2 out of 10 *(80/20)*

Now that I've specifically mentioned it, maybe three?

If that happens, three look it up instead of only two, just by a
little appeal
        in that one sentence, what happened to my "closing ratio?"
        That's what sales managers call your "batting average" that
shows the number of times you actually got the prospect to buy.

So if just one more person "bought" into looking up the word
        as I "asked" you to do,
                how powerful is that?

Don't neglect conveying your

expectations, and moving someone in the direction

you want them to go. And if you do it with passion,
        with a positive expectation, the results you want can't help
                but happen more times than if you're just going
        through the motions. Suppose I said,
        "Oh, you can look it up if you want to . . ."
How many do you suppose would look it up? Less than three?
Absolutely.
Less than two? More than likely.

I have had more than one occasion to practice my sales skills
        and corporate strategies *(especially my art of persuasion),*
        with my children.

It's easy to take a principle or strategy that works
        with people or children and apply it to business.
        And when you find you're taking those business strategies and
applying them on a level where even a small child can understand
them, you're becoming

a master craftsman in the art of

communication.

Here's another example.

Exit Strategy

A couple of years ago I had a little "father to daughter" chat
with Lindsay. It seems we had ended up with yet another "outing"
that didn't finish up with her getting home as planned or
at the appointed time. That was part of the problem, no plan.

Oh she was great at creative thinking when it came to finding a way
to "begin" . . . a night out, a trip to the mall, out to eat with friends,
whatever the impending event might be.

But once the field trip from home began,
that was the extent of her planning.
Just get things in motion and hoping somehow they'd all work out.
Or not.

So we had the chat.
I asked her if she had any idea what an "exit strategy" was.
As you might guess, she did not.

Not a lot of businesspeople know, or use one, so you would figure
a teenaged daughter might need an explanation. And she did.

I explained to her that as good as she was at creating ways to make
these fun outings happen, she was not as good
in the follow-up department (know anyone like this?).
Her ability to get to the finish line was sadly lacking.

She'd end up at someone's house or at a restaurant,
or wherever, calling me or her mom needing a ride.
Or maybe saying she was running late and was on the way, sort of.

Enter, exit strategy.

I explained that it was just as important, maybe even more so,
to finish the outing or event so we'd feel good about
the next time she had a similar request.
And that she'd not been leaving a very good taste
in our mouths when we had to bail her out
because of her poor planning. So I wanted her

to have an exit strategy planned out
before the outing began.

She understood.
From then on each time she would ask about eating outings,
mall trips, or other entertainment excursions,
I would always ask, *"What's your exit strategy?"*
And she'd have a ride or a plan or a time we could expect her
and she could arrive, safely at home.

Hey there's a valuable lesson in there for all of us. It was funny
to see the reaction of some of her friends when I asked the
exit strategy question. Lots of puzzled looks, and then
she'd explain *(teach)* the concept to them.
It's a great feeling to know that a lesson or some wisdom you tried
to impart to a student, especially a young one, made it.
Reached its destination, became a part of his or her life learning,
and you played some small part in that process.

That's why it's worth it, being a serious student.

And why I love to teach.

Speaking of friends and family, let me give you a bit of advice.

It's something I've learned over all my years of being a student.
If you ever write a book *(and I hope you will),*
make sure to include something in there about your mother!

Because if no one else ever buys a copy of your book,
    you better believe Mom's gonna get a copy.
Maybe a few copies, to hand out to all her friends with, of course,
    the obligatory *"That's my baby"* stories.

With that advice in mind,
let me introduce you to mine . . .
June Jeanette.

Hers has not been an easy life, but it has been a life with purpose
and resolve. **She's my biggest fan.** Over the years I've
    held many jobs, and a few weren't exactly mainstream
      or logical progressions to the next career step.

But if I called her tomorrow and said I'm giving up
everything I've worked for to become a student of rocket science
    or to jackhammer sidewalks or to pursue my dream of
becoming a professional fisherman/golfer . . .
know what she'd say?

"I think that's wonderful Hon!"
"You'll do great. I'm so proud of you."
Now eventually she might work her way into sharing a few
    of her concerns about the change,
      but she is, for the most part, an encourager.

I'll never forget all the times
* as a youngster when she'd drive me*
*   here, there, and everywhere.*

So I could compete in speaking
contests, or attend 4-H meetings,
or work at three different jobs
when I was 15 (and too young to drive),
and she did it without complaint.
And that, among many investments, not just in me
but in all her children, does not go unnoticed or unappreciated.

She is an amazing woman. Complex but caring.

And certainly an example of someone who has invested her life
in others to add value to her world.

Thanks Mom!

"Always do right.
This will gratify some people, and
astonish the rest."
—Mark Twain

(OH NO, NOT ANOTHER ONE . . .)
GOALS AND TARGETS

Oh no, not another book with another section on goal setting . . .
That's what those 8 out of 10 are going to be saying,
(and that's out of the 20% that are reading this in the first place)
but it is true that success leaves clues.

I have to give Mr. Ziglar a great deal of credit for my getting started
in setting goals. One of the first tape series I ever purchased
was his *Goals Program (I still have the original, over 20 years later).*
It's the three tapes and two workbooks.
I have also used his personal planner for the past several years,
before developing and printing my own line
of journals and planners.

It was Zig who planted the seeds of goal-setting in my life.
They were nurtured and fed, and I definitely saw them bear
fruit over the next several years.

But it was Jim Rohn's simple approach to goals that gave me
a new appreciation for even the simplest of goals
and how they could be achieved.

Years later, I'll never forget the first time I spoke on setting goals
and how the audience reacted to my "new and improved"
goal setting. My first goal was to
clean out the garage.
That might make you wonder a bit, but consider this.
That was a goal I absolutely knew that I could accomplish . . .
if I only would. Meaning if I really wanted it and went
to work on it. So sure enough, that next Saturday morning,
I tackled the garage. *Eureka!* It really worked.
I did it.

Get out that list of goals and check that one off.
On to goal #2 . . . and so on it went.
It's another of those power principles,
    or in this case it's actually a law.
        The Law of Inertia. Remember this one?
            You know, the one that says that a body in motion
            (once it is actually in motion), tends to stay in motion,
                and a body at rest, *(all too often the case)* tends to remain at rest.

Wow! Talk about the power of simplicity.
But after all, it is the law.

When you begin to apply your efforts in the direction of a goal, or a task, you seem to

acquire this drive, this motion that carries you to desired results.
    And selling a certain dollar volume,
        creating a new spirit of cooperation in your team, increasing
    your time reading and writing,
            or just cleaning out the garage, can be achieved.

How simple is Setting Goals? Try this . . .
1. Decide what you want
2. Write it all down
3. Save the old lists *(revise as you progress)*
4. Check off the items *(start small)*
5. Put little things and big things on your list
6. Set the kind of goals that will make something of <u>YOU</u>!

Those things that will make you stretch and make you grow.
That will allow you to be pulled in the direction of your dreams.
    It's an amazing thing, how this process moves you to results.
It's like putting up the sail on your ship, and when life's winds
    catch the sails, you are propelled in the direction you desire.
        It's a simple process. It's fairly easy to do.

So why don't more people do it? It's easier not to do,
and most people have never experienced the power of the process.

Another of those early goals was to

read 4 new books a month.

Just four. That's only one a week.
Notice I didn't specify that it had to be a
100-page paperback like *Life Is Tremendous,*
or a *War and Peace*-type novel. Just 4 new books.

Know what happened?
Well, first of all I didn't achieve my goal . . . every month.
But I did see the law at work. Just going into a library or bookstore
got me excited about books and about building my library,
and about reading those four new books.

Once I started, began the motion, in a direction, it became . . .
well, easier.
I could feel myself being drawn in the direction of my goal.
I tried to set aside some time each week for a bookstore visit.
Or if I was a little short on discretionary income, the library.

Now there's some buried treasure—THE LIBRARY! It's like
BOOKS4FREE.com . . .
Remember the statistic we talked about earlier,
that only about 3% of Americans own a library card?
Does that tell you something? 3%!
That 3% must certainly be uncommon.

So why don't more people use the library?
Thousands and thousands of books, on almost any subject, including
success stories, instruction on life, business and, yes, even sales
and goal-setting, all right there in the library
*(It's almost like **money4free.com**).*

And "the law" works in the library too.
You don't just check out one book,
you find yourself leaving with three or four or more.
Amazing isn't it? But it is the law . . .
the law of inertia. Try it.

When I began to set goals for good

(and it will be for your good when you really begin setting them),
I broke them down into periods of time that I could measure,
evaluate, review, and even revise.

Some were easy, like the garage. Some were harder, and that's OK
because that makes you grow. I've found it's true that
stretching for goals does make you grow. Some goals were daily,
to do every day. An easy one for that category is . . . well, to get up.

Let's face it. Eventually we all have to get up.
That's a little loosely defined though, wouldn't you say?
Maybe, get up by nine . . . or, if you really want to stretch,
get up at dawn.
GET UP AT DAWN???? *Are you kidding?*
No, I did say, get up at dawn.

This looks like a good time for a story . . .

Because of goal setting, I happened to win a trip with
The Woman . . . uh, that's what I call my lovely bride of 24 years.
Her name is Sandi, but her hair is red,
and when I speak to her, or sometimes of her, she is simply . . .
The Woman. Anyway, The Woman and I
win this trip along with 2 other couples to Tryall Resort,
in Jamaica. It's a gorgeous old sugar plantation house
sitting on a hilltop just off the beach.
It is surrounded by a magnificent golf course that once
hosted the Johnnie Walker World Championships. The course
wraps around the "Great House" as it's called and, with
the beaches below, provides some magnificent views.

Tryall is just a short distance away from Montego Bay and the first
morning the guys were going to get in a round of golf before noon.

That meant up early and at the first tee by 7.

Now with that schedule, my goal was, obviously, UP EARLY! Let's say dawn. As I rolled out of bed that morning it was still dark, and I took my shoes outside the French doors that open to a private veranda surrounded by red hibiscus in full bloom.

As I sat there quietly putting on my shoes, the sun began to peek over Montego Bay. The first rays of light glistened off the water, then through the palm trees and across the freshly mown grass of the fairways and greens.

It was incredible!

So was the golf. Not necessarily the scores, but you could hit a bad shot, take three steps in any direction, and forget all about the bad shot.

The scenery was breathtaking, color bursting everywhere, the blues of the ocean, the golden sands, the greens of the trees, and the rainbow of different flowers. Unforgettable.

We were there for six days.
Guess how many days I got up BEFORE dawn?
That's right. All of them. After that first sunrise experience, I had to drink in as many as I could.
So while I could have slept as late as I wanted, my goal was not to miss one single sunrise over Montego Bay. Check that one off the list.
Goal accomplished. Once again, the law prevails.

So even if a goal seems easy, it should be well-defined.

If you're starting a new job, a good goal would be to accelerate the learning curve, high-gear, fast-track *(we'd call that fast forward),* lots of activity. Make any calls or contacts that can help get you up to speed in your new position. Use resources available to you *(like the library)* and relationships you have with business contacts or friends as "partners" *(to give input, feedback, etc.).*

Seek out successes around you and ask questions with a purpose.

All of these are things that are important in the first days and weeks.
Then there's the larger units of measure . . . 10-day goals
(Then evaluate your progress), 30-day, 90-day, 6 months, 1 year and so on
(skip 60, it'll give you a larger accomplishment window).

An Uncommon Tip on Goal-Setting

An easy way of getting started with goal-setting is to write a letter. To someone, almost anyone, even yourself; and date it one year from today. Write about all the things you've done and seen and accomplished in the past year. It'll get you thinking about goals in a real-life, "I believe it can happen" frame of mind.

Make a list of things you'd like to do and see. And no matter where you are in your career and your life you can make a list of your victories and accomplishments to date.

Go on. It'll build your confidence, plus it gets inertia's law working for you. Also list all the places you've been and the things you've enjoyed doing. I keep my list handy so I can reflect on those special times and throw another log on the "great memories" fire.

"In the long run, men hit mostly what they aim at."

—Thoreau

Remember goal setting is a process you can learn
with just a little practice in the right direction.

It's easier than believing you could hold that bicycle upright
without the training wheels . . . and just look how that turned out.
On the next page you'll see a blank sample of a goal contract.

It's a contract you make with yourself.

Don't use it until you've been riding without the training wheels
for a while and you're ready to make a commitment to yourself.

Goal Contract

Date _____

This day I commit my energies to my success.

I will design and plan for uncommon results.
By *(this date)*

I will

(whatever you're going to do . . . your goal or objective)

I will enjoy the rewards of my accomplishments.

For I will earn them as a result of giving the best effort and service
I can provide to the marketplace in the capacity of
(ad salesperson, speaker, whatever)

This is an irrevocable contract I make with myself.
I will persist until I succeed.

*(Put one of your favorite quotes or inspirational messages here
to help you stay focused and committed.)*

Signed _____

This is just a sample of the kinds of written commitments you can
make with YOU!
The most powerful contract you'll ever agree to
is the one you make with yourself
to do something incredible.

Give it a try.

Success leaves clues, and there are many mysteries.
Do you know the answer to this one?

I am

Your constant companion.

I am your greatest helper or toughest obstacle.
I will push you onward or drag you down to failure.
I am completely at your command.

Half the things you do
might just as well be turned over to me,
and I will do them almost effortlessly and correctly.

I am easily managed.
You must merely be firm with me in the beginning,
and consistent with me for a time.
Show me exactly how you want something done,
and after a few lessons, I will take over and do it
almost automatically.

I am the servant of all great people and alas,
of all failures as well. Those great, I have made great.
And those who fail, I have made failures.

I am not a machine, though I work with the ease of one,
and have the intelligence of a person just like you.
You may use me for profit or for ruin, it makes no difference to me.

Take me, teach me, be firm with me, and I will place the best
things in life at your disposal. Ignore me or treat me carelessly,
and I will bring destruction to you.

Who am I?

For the answer to this mystery, look on the next page . . .

Who am I?

I am HABIT.

Go back and read it one more time and see how this clue
fits into the success puzzle. It's a critical piece.

Good habits and bad habits are cultivated or developed
   by each of us. Unique or common, productive or destructive,
we each have the power to choose.

Which habit that you've developed are you most pleased about?

Which one causes you the greatest concern?

If there's something about you, or about your life,
   that you'd like to change, then go to work on
   changing the habits that can bring them to pass.

It's easy to do.
But it's easier not to do.

Which one do you choose?

"Do all the good you can,
   by all the means you can,
      in all the ways you can,
         in all the places you can,
      at all the times you can,
         to all the people you can,
            as long as ever you can."
—John Wesley

YOU'RE A GOOD PERSON

Once in a while something happens in a corporate environment
    that really wows me!
        Now when you're in an entrepreneurial
environment you get wowed a lot, but not as often in
        the bureaucratic, traditional old-school business setting.

Someone whom I consider a friend, and worked closely with
for a time, was in a management position with little *(or no)* positive
    reinforcement and under tremendous stress to get the job done
        to the satisfaction of "the board"
            (the higher ups, the big man, up the ladder).

"These are the times that try men's souls,"
someone once said about the kind of situation she was facing.
We'll call her Jesse *(not her real name),*
                and most of the messages that came down the
            ladder were less than encouraging or inspiring, typically
                something about being on the radar screen,
or worse, and having to make the numbers . . . *(gulp)* or else!

Ever been in a situation like that?
You sometimes have a tendency to lose perspective, lose sight
    of what's really important. After all, these are the times when
    lots of executives or salespeople or workers crumble,
        or ignore most things *(other than work)* that should be
    really important to them.

So how the "wow?"
Jesse sent me an email she had received from up the ladder
    that was maybe one of the most powerful I've ever seen
from upper management. The gentleman was relatively new to
    the company but had gotten to know Jesse and her family.

He had also been in several meetings with Jesse and witnessed firsthand the crucible of pressure that she was facing.

Dan was not her supervisor, or even in the same division of the company, but he took it upon himself to send Jesse a message right out of the blue.

The message was simple and to the point . . .

Under the subject of the memo, it read simply . . . "life."
Then followed these words:

Hi Jesse,

You are a good person. You have a nice family, and a good marriage. You are good at what you do. These are the things that matter.

Hang in there,
Dan

Wow . . .
I mean, WOW!

Jesse called me and said she had just gotten the most unique message, and I believe she described it perfectly.

Unique. Uncommon.

A powerful encouragement with dramatic style.
And the truth.

Last I heard, Jesse was still in her position with the company, still facing the heat, and still with a nice family and a good marriage.

I'm so glad there are still guys like Dan in the ranks of corporate America's upper management.
Thanks Dan.

"How far you go in life depends on you being tender with the young, compassionate with the aged, sympathetic with the striving and tolerant of the weak and the strong.

Because someday in life you will have been all of these."

—George Washington Carver

Everybody sells something!

Several years ago I was in Nashville, Tennessee, to address a regional
meeting of salespeople for a company I was working with.

As I waited in the hallway of this giant hotel to take my turn on
the platform I was reading from a beautiful display case which held
   many collectibles, paintings, and writings on the game of golf.

Positioned at the top of the display case was a bronze plaque
   with the following words etched upon it:

The Magnificent Game of Skill.

While they were obviously addressing the qualities
   and characteristics of golf,
      I was reflecting on how that also described
         the profession of selling. And whenever I speak or write,
I often refer to what some people call "sales"
      as something that we should all look at on a grander scale.

This "profession" is one we can be proud of.
It is a game, and certainly a magnificent one.
One that requires a greater degree of skill than ever before
   to truly succeed.

When I took the platform that day, I couldn't help but
   make reference to what I had seen in the hallway of that hotel.
   It's a reference I have made many times since that day.

And I believe it to be just as true today and for the future.

Our challenge is to study our craft
with the diligence of
a medical student preparing to be a doctor
or a future attorney preparing for the bar exam.
There is most certainly an art to selling, the art of persuasion.

At its highest level it requires the utmost skill,
yet is made to appear almost effortless.
That my friends is the magnificent game of skill
that I love, the profession of selling.

Make no mistake, sales is a game. Just like life is a game.
How are you playing it?
There's a song that I used to play on the radio
in my younger disc jockey days.
It's by Jim Seals and Dash Crofts. *(remember Seals & Crofts?)*
The song's called *We May Never Pass This Way Again.*

The words of one of the verses . . . *"Life, so they say,*
is but a game, and they'd let it
slip away . . ."

Sad, but true. Life is a game; let's play it.
Embrace it, grab it for all you're worth, and hold on.
Big events, small moments, get your arms around them.
Write them down, take pictures of them,
and savor the memories.
Relish the victories and grow from the failures.

What is a Sales *Professional?*

Why do you suppose not everyone holds this profession
in the same high esteem?
Let's investigate.

What comes to mind when the average individual thinks of sales or a salesperson?

I've posed this question to many audiences and the answers are always the same . . .

"Say anything . . .
Do anything . . . Pushy . . . Obnoxious . . .
Less than truthful . . ."
WOW, isn't that the kind of profession young people must be clamoring to be a part of?

I love the TV commercial with all the kids staring into the camera with this deadpan-style delivery,
"When I grow up I want to be forced into early retirement," or
"Be paid less for doing the same job," and on and on it goes.
Not exactly inspirational stuff, but it gets the point across.

Perception is the basis for most initial communication with salespeople, or anyone else for that matter.

A less-than-trustworthy or *"position of risk"* perspective is why so many salespeople feel rejection. It's just a logical response to the type of perception that has been created when dealing with those *"fast-talking salesman types."*
The communication from the other side of the desk is cautious, and the deflector shields are up!
If you want to be uncommon in this area always begin with the truth and build from there.

"If the truth isn't enough,
then you must become stronger
at presenting it."

—Jim Rohn

What if we, as salespeople or just as communicators, could remove the risk? Could help ease that "fear" or risk *(real or imagined)* felt by the other person?

I was having a late-afternoon lunch recently before one of my seminars, and while I perused the menu an energetic young man appeared at my table,

"Hi, I'm Dave," he said as he flashed a big smile and asked,
"What can I get you to drink on this fine day, sir?"
I smiled back, "I'll have a tall iced tea, Dave."

"Great choice.
    Do you need a minute, or do you know what you want?"
I told him I might need a minute.
I wanted something kind of light since I'd be speaking for
    a couple of hours soon and didn't want to go on stage too full.

Dave says,
"Well, if I could make a suggestion . . .
Our newest item is our Greek salad with grilled chicken strips.
It's in our own dressing and people have really seemed to like it."

That did sound good. And as I began to include that option in my
    decision-making process, Dave said something magical . . .
"And if you don't like it
    for whatever reason . . .
        I'LL TAKE IT BACK!"

Huh?
Dave, what did you just say?
You'd take it back?

He said it with a smile, but I could tell he wasn't kidding.
        And almost before I could process that information
        I found myself saying,
"Great, I'll take the Greek salad."

Dave was an outstanding waiter. And an exceptional communicator.
He obviously loved his work *(he'd been there for 4 years . . . I asked)*
        and made me enjoy eating in his restaurant.

But the best thing Dave did in that little "selling" session
                        was to *remove the risk.*

Major Key:
Remove the Risk and Everybody Wins.

Dave did not have to take the salad back.
It was delicious.
I doubt that he takes back many, if any, of his suggested dishes
        due to his customers being less than satisfied.

Just by the fact that he removed the bit of uncertainty
        or indecision I was feeling at the time, I ended up not getting
        a cup of soup or what I thought was my first choice . . .
but something I really enjoyed that was brand-new.
        Something that I'd never tried, or maybe never would
        have thought to, without Dave's suggestion and risk-removal.
Wow.

Not to mention I spent twice as much on that entree
as I would have on the soup.

Sound like pretty good results from uncommon customer service?

Increased revenues.
        Enthusiastic service.
                Happy customer.

And of course, a larger-than-usual tip for Dave.

Because as one uncommon friend and business partner of mine
says . . .
*"We don't believe in tipping — we believe in
OVER-tipping!"*
(Thanks Mark.)
And Thanks Dave.

Be on guard.
Great lessons on life and business are wherever you find them.
Whether you realize it or not,
daily you create a reputation that people speak about to others.
That happens in life, as well as in the profession of selling.

So develop your character and give the people who know you the
opportunity to spread that word-of-mouth advertising that
makes others want to be around you, even be like you
and do business with you.
Can you change the perception of sales and . . . SALESPEOPLE?
Sure you can. That's exactly how it's done, one salesperson at a time.

Why not Honest . . . has Integrity . . . Dependable . . . Professional . . . ?
Wouldn't that be an uncommon perception of a salesperson?
You know what they say about perception and reality.
And at least 8 out of 10 people *(even more now)* who attempt
to make their living in the arena of sales are making the perception
of obnoxious, pushy, anything-but-the-truth,
anything-for-a-buck salesperson, a reality.
Sad but true. So what's the answer?

A lot of what we've discussed here about increasing value,
establishing principles, and creating a solid foundation
that you can build on applies to life just as much as it
applies to sales. That should include honesty, integrity,
dependability, reputation as a professional,
you know, those integrity kinds of things.

So now you have the good news and the bad news!
If I ask you, "How can you then set yourself apart
     from the stereotype of salesmen?"
          How can you stand out from the crowd as an honest, trusted,
     valued confidant of your customers and be perceived as
a true SALES PROFESSIONAL?

One of my early sales jobs was with a daily newspaper.
I came into a selling situation that I knew very little about.
     I was not familiar with the product,
          coming from a radio background, and I was only 25,
but determined to succeed.

At that newspaper I met one of the managers
     who affected change in me the most.
Dave Reddoch had a style that was quiet and unassuming.
He was never loud or intimidating but could convey his expectations
          to you in a way that would make you want to do it
          for him . . . and for you!
I still keep in touch with Dave today,
and Dave is still affecting lives *(young and old alike)* in his work
     all these years later.
Thanks Dave.

In just over a year in that new position, I took a small territory
doing around a quarter of a million in business and doubled it!
     "WOW! Superman, we found him," they must have thought.

But in reality, it became clear to me that the guy I
replaced in my newspaper sales position was coasting.
     In fact he couldn't have been working more than
          two days a week.
          Because even with all the goofy mistakes I made,
               just based on a 4.5 day work week
               (a half day to do paperwork and plan my week) of calling on
               advertising prospects and getting face to face with
               as many people as I could see, sales went up. Dramatically!

I was a hero, and my confidence soared.
The next year I won a sales contest, sending me and my wife
    to Southern California!
        Disneyland, Hollywood, the whole
            "way to go, spoils of victory" thing.

And what almost no one could believe is that this "new kid"
        beat out THE BEST!
        A 13-year sales veteran who had all the big, cherry accounts!

That's one of my earliest ***"Fast Forward"*** experiences.

"Fast Forward" is one of the phrases, or mottos, that we used
to challenge one another in many of the selling situations I was in.

Both as an aspiring sales professional and later
    as a Director of Sales challenging a team.
Fast Forward! It means *"let's go, let's get on with it."*
        It was, and is, an action phrase that basically says
        let's make it happen.

I stayed for five years at that newspaper.
Eventually I moved into a management role and into
start-up projects that needed to go from ground zero to big results,
and oh yes, *"How soon can you get there?"*

    That's always the question from up the ladder isn't it?
We don't have a lot of time, how soon can we see the results?

Is that what I mean by Fast Forward? Not exactly.
        There absolutely must be a foundation for the
individual, the team, the company.

Otherwise sooner or later any progress will find the same fate
    as the house with that quick-fix foundation.

Fast Forward is not about short-cuts,
it's about advancing solidly in the direction you desire.
Can you imagine a builder saying to his crew
"OK, just skip the foundation and let's go right to the house.
These people gotta be moved in here soon,
so we can't waste any time."
How long do you suppose that structure would stand
without a solid foundation?

Everyone wants to see that 40-story building jump out of the ground
and climb to the sky, but the value an architect brings to that vision
is a plan and a solid foundation.

Ridiculous, isn't it, the very thought of a structure of any kind enduring without a strong foundation.

Yet that's exactly how many companies,
and even individuals, build their businesses and careers.
They want to get to the good part.

The parades, the balloons, the big commissions and bonuses,
that *"Sales Maker of the Year"* plaque . . .

One of the great life lessons here is from the script
that tells of two men. They're even described
by their actions, as foolish and wise.

The story goes that the foolish man built his house on the sand.
Little thought of planning or foundation was given to the
construction. And the winds blew, and the rains came

and the house simply could not stand.

No structure, or individual, can last for long
in the face of adversity without solid planning and principles
that make up the foundation.

The wise man knew this.

The story says he built his house on the rock. And the same storms, and winds and rains came; but the wise man's house stood firm.

That's "rock-solid" principles in action.

A strong foundation is not a step you want to skip, especially if you want to be referred to as the wise one in someone's story.

So let the house that was built on the solid foundation be just like your career, your company, or your life. One that will stand the tests, and the storms, of time.

You can build it, and then build it bigger, because of the foundational principles and building blocks you put in place in the beginning.

It's hard, and it's easy.

"It's easy to do, but it's <u>easier</u> not to do!"

When you think about what that really means, if we do things the right way, it will be easy to stand out.

To be different.

We'll get noticed.

Isn't that uncommon?

Major Key:
Don't Neglect Doing the Things in Life
That Are Easy to Do.

Because that means they're easy to miss. Easier not to do.

So don't settle for the EASIER things, *just do the things that are easy.* You'll be amazed at the uncommon things that can happen.

SELL ON!

No matter how the "newest" new economy shapes our futures,
there will always be a need for men and
women who choose the profession of selling
as their enterprise.

To move goods and services,
to establish relationships,
to solve, to consult, to instruct.

When you do, you prepare yourself for a day in the future
when you may well choose to join the ranks of the entrepreneur,
having a business of your very own
and providing jobs for others.

That's really how a sales professional should view himself anyway,
as a provider of products to the marketplace.

Compensated for the value you give and bring
to the world of commerce.

"Free enterprise
means that the more enterprising you are,
the freer you are."
—Mark Victor Hansen

A MILLION-DOLLAR COACH

Andrew Carnegie was successful on many scales of measure.
As a person, businessman, instructor, goal-setter, and more.

Andrew Carnegie, the steel baron and philanthropist who funded America's 3,000 libraries and the great Carnegie Hall.
At one point Mr. Carnegie had 43 millionaires under his employ.

How'd you like to have 43 millionaires working for you or even with you?

Is it possible? Sure is; it's already been done.
You don't have to set the precedent, just find out about the model.
When asked in a newspaper interview how in the world he
managed to have 43 millionaires working for him,
Mr. Carnegie smiled and said simply,
"None of them were millionaires when I hired them."

Bang! Did you get that? A million-dollar coach.
A million-dollar teacher. A model for millionaires,
that was Andrew Carnegie.

Would you guess that someone of this stature in life and business might set goals?

So would I. And we'd, of course, be right.

When Mr. Carnegie died he was found to have among his personal effects in his office a piece of paper with some notes and
thoughts he had written down. One of these was a
long-range goal, and it read something like this:
*"I want to spend the first half of my life becoming rich.
And I want to spend the second half of my life giving it all away."*
GIVING IT ALL AWAY?
Could that really be someone's goal in life,
to give away a fortune they'd spent half their life to achieve?
And the answer is, of course.
And that is exactly what Mr. Carnegie did.

He became rich in so many more ways than just his money.

He taught and mentored dozens to follow his example to wealth,
in business and life. And he used his fortune
to impact the world around him in so many ways.
Mr. Carnegie is also responsible, directly or indirectly,
for what we know today as
personal development books and tapes.
It was his commission of a young writer by the name of
Napoleon Hill that brought about the book *Think and Grow Rich*,
a book that has gone through an amazing 43 printings
(and maybe even more by now).
Hill spoke with countless individuals on success and the secret
of that success. *It's an amazing story* and one which,
if you've never had the pleasure of reading, you should read soon.
Few success libraries can be considered complete without this
Napoleon Hill classic. And it all started with Andrew Carnegie.

My challenge to you is to find out more about this man.
Wouldn't you like to know more about his life, his principles,
his clues to success? Surely we all would,
but where could we find such a thing?

It's your local library *(thanks Mr. Carnegie),* and
tomorrow you can get in for free.
No admission charge.
Information and instruction. Inspiration and human drama,
yours for the taking. I should tell you that even as easy as
that would be to do, how many do you think will take the
initiative to find out for themselves?
Sadly, not enough. Don't be one of them. Get the books and tapes
and seek out the clues success has left just for you.

*"Always bear in mind
that your own resolution to succeed is
more important than any other one thing."*
—Abraham Lincoln

The greater the explosion of technology,
>   the greater the need, the demand, for talent.
For dynamic "impact" people.

Building Talent

As a Director of Sales, and later as a *Talent Consultant*,
>   I have interviewed hundreds of individuals.
Most for sales-related positions, some for other department heads,
>   a few were administrative or support positions.
I've even been in on the interview process to find my replacement
>   in a couple of instances.

What I've learned over all those years is to take a different view
of what most companies and organizations call recruiting.
>   The military recruits. College coaches recruit.
>   And most of us have at one time been "recruited" for some
network marketing company by a friend or
>   someone we didn't even know.

Recruiting should not be the mission for most organizations.
Attracting talent is the goal.
>   The talent pool in the marketplace is unprecedented.
Companies have been "forced" to downsize thousands and
thousands of talented individuals, turning them onto the streets.

As these "free agents" begin their search for their next position
>   or career, many of them do so with a different mind-set.

They may now consider things that before this transition
>   they would not have looked at in the same light.

Many of these talented individuals can be attracted to
>   a new position and a new organization, if that organization
>   develops a process that attracts talent with
a genuine opportunity . . .

And then employs the four keys to "uncommon" we
discussed earlier, sharing a vision with powerful communication.
(Have you heard? We're going to the moon!)

"Image is the sum of beliefs, ideas, and impressions."
So says the strategic marketing office for nonprofit organizations.
Hmmm. Consider that for just a moment; what if it's true?
In today's marketplace, it is.
Words matter, actions matter, visuals matter, results matter!
What we say, how we say it, what we do,
and what happens as a result of what we do.

The Colonial Advantage

Over the past year I have had the opportunity to work as a consultant
with a national insurance company in the area of talent building.
Attracting and developing new, and to some degree, existing talent.
Specifically, to work within a designated region
of the company, in a sort of "pilot program."

I share this story with you here not to say *"Hey, look at what I did,"*
but to show you how we did it together and made a difference.
Working with Lou has been an uncommon experience.
Lou is a managing general agent with Colonial in a territory
that was under-performing according to the company
goals and projections, primarily in new business.

Colonial is a class organization.
They aren't your typical insurance company,
they specialize in voluntary benefits, supplemental coverages
that enhance an employee's regular medical insurance.
But the really impressive thing about Colonial is how they do it.

How they do it at the home office level with efficiency and a real
service mentality among the team.
And how they do it in the field by delivering
"benefits communication."
Assisting companies and organizations in creating an understanding
of the benefits the employer provides for their employees.

It's a much-needed service, and really has less to do with the products they provide *(most supplemental products are the same for any company)* and lots to do with how they handle the process.

It is uncommon.

Even uncommon organizations are faced with challenges
as the marketplace changes.
And Colonial is no different.
Company-wide, and specifically in Lou's division,
not enough new agents were coming on board, and of those,
not enough were developing new business.

Many of the "tenured" agents who'd been around for awhile, had built a block of business and had their hands full taking care of that business, leaving little or no time to pursue new cases or create any real momentum in the marketplace that generated new revenues.

After joining this organization in a consulting role, I explored lots of issues and decided the best and most productive direction would be to focus on changing the way
Colonial attracts and builds talent.

And focus on improving the way new agents were
developed, building a culture that would equip, prepare,
and challenge them to succeed immediately. We put the emphasis not on training but on learning. Creating a learning environment and providing inspiration as well as instruction.

Colonial was in the process of developing "role specialization"
company-wide, and the role we wanted to develop was called the "opener" role.
Initially we debated on changing the name, coming up with a new designation for this "special" agent. Ultimately though we decided to keep the name and develop a new "brand" of opener.

An Opener with a capital "O!"

A sign of distinction.

We would create a new brand of agent.
A distinctive talent that did one thing, and did that one thing
extremely well. We would also create a culture within
the organization that celebrated opening!

We determined that "Opener" perfectly described this position.
It was different from the old-school "closers" most sales
organizations talked about.
This class of individual would be opening new relationships
and helping provide solutions to human resources while getting
top officers of the company to be "open-minded" about
Colonial's advantages over other insurance companies
and supplemental providers.

It was *(and continues to prove)* challenging.
I took my ideas and developed new tools for Openers.
Including a new way of looking at this position.
The Opener, the ultimate agent, boldly goes into the marketplace
to cultivate new accounts *(cases)* and increases
new business revenues. We also needed a new way of attracting
this type of individual with the qualities we were looking for.

So I sat down to write a document called *The Opener Creed.*
To identify what the ideal, qualities, and characteristics
of the individual should be.
I've included it here so you can see that we put an emphasis
on the individual and not just on their skills and abilities.

Because you can't be one kind of person
and be a different kind of worker, you are the
same personally and professionally. With the same fundamentals,
philosophies, and ideals that shape your thoughts and actions.

The Opener Creed

I am an aspiring professional,
   with the passion, heart, and determination of a Top Performer.

It is my goal to work in a professional environment.
To have fun with and respect those around me.
      To attack my work with a passion that will prove to others
that I am an uncommon individual.

I do not belong with the masses, for I have chosen a business of independence.
      I am a captain of enterprise in a nation of opportunity.

I will be a continuous learner and not depend on the crutch of experience nor rest
on the successes of the past, for my greatest achievements are ahead.
I will strive daily to do professional work in a professional way,
      producing dynamic results that will transform my life in the process.

I will strive to consistently be INSPIRED about my life and my work.
      I will be strong and courageous, LOVE PEOPLE, and lead by EXAMPLE.
I will take RESPONSIBILITY for how things work out
      and will accept neither PRAISE nor MONEY that is not DESERVED.

I will create value, educate business leaders, and build CONFIDENCE
      in those around me.
I will BE HONEST with others and with myself. I will RISK NEW IDEAS and
      build a foundation of IDEALS and FUNDAMENTALS that are
      UNSHAKEABLE!

I will share this opportunity with others
      in appreciation for those who once shared it with me.

This is The Future and I will help make it great for me,
my family, my company, and my customers.

I am an *OPENER.*

BECOME A TALENT MAGNET

By putting this message out to talent in the marketplace that we wanted to attract, they in turn became attracted to an organization that put a premium on them as uncommon individuals.

And because they've worked harder on themselves over the years *(work harder on you than you do on your job)*, they'll be able to perform any task better because they have the right fundamentals and foundations we're looking for.

Guess how many organizations work at attracting talent this way? Answer: not enough.

How are you attracting talent to your organization?
What magnet are you using?
Recruiting?
Blah, blah, blah. *"We do this and that and the other thing . . ."*

Uncommon companies have always known it's easier to attract talent to the organization than to continually seek and search for talent and then have to sell them on your position or opportunity.

When talent is attracted to Disney or Southwest Airlines or other uncommon organizations, the individual has already decided in many cases that this is a team they'd love to be a part of.

So how can you do it?
There are lots of ways to do it.
Here's how we did it.

Our first challenge was to "sell" this new idea and our new Opener strategy to all of Lou's managers.
I can still recall the first time I addressed them in a formal meeting.
Lou and I had been having meeting sessions for many weeks, but this was the first time for me to speak to the collective group, and I knew it would be a challenge.

No one wants to change just for the sake of change,
    especially when they've been through changes
        that didn't improve things or didn't work. Many of
    these managers were doing well in a "maintenance" mode,
maintaining a block of business and doing well financially.

There is often little you can say or do to interest anyone
in radical growth and improvement for the organization
    when things are going well for them personally.
    Even though most any organization needs new growth,
        all managers may not. Or may not recognize it.

That's a major key, that they
recognize and focus on continuing improvement.
        Not just to be content with a "maintaining" position.

And to compound the problem of perception, here was a guy
    being brought in *(me)* who knew almost nothing about the
insurance business . . . as a consultant to help build their business.
Challenging stuff.

I showed them a quote from Ted Turner that said when he bought
the Atlanta Braves he didn't know the difference between a balk
and an infield fly *(he wasn't a baseball expert with years of ownership experience),*
        but "I do have the ability to inspire people," Turner said.
    He calls it "executive ability."
Cool. That was my goal, to inspire people,
    to bring a fresh perspective and new ideas.
To prove we could change the opener role and by doing so,
        change the results.

Lou started that meeting by introducing me as an "odd" kind of guy.
(I'll never let him forget that one.)
        "I mean he's different," Lou explained.
And when the familiar isn't working, different is worth trying.
        (Being just 10 or 15% better would be considered a miserable failure.)
    The sessions went well, and we began the process
            of radical, dynamic improvement.

After much deliberation, I came up with a concept for
a two-day Opener school called "COOL $chool."

At first I thought it might be a little "out there" for a company
that had been around for over 60 years in the insurance business.
But it was Lou who convinced me that it was the right move.
It was also his suggestion to hold the school at the home office,
to showcase the people and resources available
to the Opener in the field.

COOL was "Colonial Opener Opportunity Launch."
If words matter *(and they do)*, these meant something,
or we wanted them to mean something, to the new agent.

First things first.
I wanted this school to be COOL!
To be different.
Atypical and unconventional.
Uncommon.

It was designed to be a "learning" challenge and not just a
training class. As we've already discussed, there is a
huge difference between learning and training, and
I wanted to convey that message to these new agents.
We added the $ to School, as an indicator that you'd generate
more $, for the company, and for you, by attending this school.

I should mention that some training classes in the organization
are required, but this one is optional.
It's specifically designed for the Opener and to be different.
It's free to the new agent, but their manager has to pay
a tuition fee and for hotel stays.

We also allow the managers to attend at no charge
(as many times as they like) to accompany their new-found talent
and to advertise the value in this "optional" school.

That's a great test for any class or instruction, if it's optional
and it costs something— after six, seven, or eight of them,
do they still come?

Do they still pay?

And do you still get good reviews and results from graduates
who are now having success in the marketplace?

We did. And still do.

We also wanted to create a sense of urgency for the new agent to
succeed . . . radically, dynamically, and NOW!

The learning curve was straight up!

Go!

So the name COOL came about as a challenge . . .

"Colonial Opener Opportunity Launch."

Launch being the operative word.

To Launch! To take off with great force;
that was the message to the attendees of this unique school.

We developed a culture around the Opener.

Creating a new "brand" awareness, or what the Opener would
be known for.

We also established COOL Tools to provide for the agent
after our school, including regular conference calls,
a website, newsletter, and a new way of presenting the
opportunity to the marketplace
(not as an insurance salesman, but as a professional services provider).

We developed contests, rewards, and recognition specifically for
Openers.

And how did it all work out?

The results have been pretty amazing.

After about eight months of having this new program in place,
there are numerous signs that Lou's territory is growing and
our Opener strategy is working. Consistent new revenue growth,
and radical success for a number of new Openers
in just their first few weeks and I'm expanding my role
into other regions.

But maybe the most telling statistic is that the number of new cases and new premiums more than doubled over the previous year . . .
in only eight months!
And we've created a momentum that will carry even greater results,
geometrically, in the weeks and months *(even years)* ahead.

In a recent letter, Lou described the successes and, in the areas of measure that matter most *(new cases, new talent in the role of Opener, etc.)*,
projected increases year over year from
between 150% to 1000% in some areas.
Wow, that sounds like radical, dynamic improvement.
The kind of results that any consultant loves to see for a client.

And not too bad from a guy who's "odd"
(a common perception of uncommon behavior).

Radical, dynamic improvement is available
if you're willing to explore the possibilities.
Thanks Lou.
Openers Rock!

A large part of our success is that we treated this situation as a
PROJECT!

Tom Peters says "all work is project work."

All work *should* be project work, but it isn't.
*Most individuals and organizations don't know
the beginning from the middle on any given day.*
Everything just sort of all runs together.
People keep showing up for work, talking about how busy they are,
and nothing ever really gets accomplished.
Any task or objective or result that needs to be achieved
should be viewed as a project.

In the beginning it's high activity, doing more than you're
    paid to do. Whether you're an employee or entrepreneur
    or consultant. It's the same reason the space shuttle
needs most of its fuel just to clear the launch pad.
    It's creating inertia, beginning the forward or upward thrust.
And it takes major energy and effort to get off to a good start.

Lots of things go on in the middle of a project, like
    evaluating progress, reviewing, revising, strategy, action, etc.

And then there has to be an ending.
A conclusion of a project so that we can celebrate our success.
    Remember, that's another of the keys to uncommon for
individuals and organizations. Celebrate accomplishment.

It shouldn't be just one long continuing J-O-B where you never
    know when you're finished or when you win *(or if you won . . . or lost)*.
    That's why most all athletic competitions are "time sensitive."
So you know where your are in the game.

It's why we have scoreboards.
    So you know how much time is left for achieving this goal.
        And you know the score, or how you're doing at
        this particular stage of the game.

It's also why so much scoring and action happens in the
final minutes of a quarter or half or game. The *"2-minute warning"*
    brings about different strategies. Two-minute offenses and
prevent defenses. By knowing the score and the time remaining,
        you can make adjustments during "your project" as well.

Many companies use "scorecards," but that usually is
        a reflection of what's already happened.
By the time scores or information make it to a scorecard,
the game's over. You can use it to review, but the competition
                or event has already passed.

Much like a golfer's scorecard, which shows, *"If I hadn't made that double bogey on 17, I would have won the tournament."*

Develop the "scoreboard" concept for you and your team and

adjust your performance based on where you are (results) at any given time in the game (your project).

Know the difference between scoreboards and scorecards and

how they can help you
on any project or objective.

Begin to attack objectives as projects,
and create the resources you need to "make it happen."
Try developing some result or objective you seek as a project
for a team to accomplish, and see how it works for you.

*"You can't build a reputation
on what you're going to do."*
—Henry Ford

4 QUESTIONS

No matter what we're engaged in, personally or as an organization,
I've found there a few questions we should always be asking
   if we want to improve dramatically.

They are easy to ask, if it's for you individually,
   your personal performance, you should ask them with an "**I**."
   And if they're for an organization or a group,

     ask them from a "**we**" perspective.
Here they are.

Number 1.
What are you doing?
Sounds easy enough, but most people never really identify
   the objective. I mean clearly identify it.
What results would make this project or objective a big success?
What are you doing here? Day-to-day, week-to-week,
     what you're engaged in on a regular basis.
     Then go to work on the answer. When you've finished,
   next question . . .

Number 2.
What SHOULD you be doing?
If you've identified exactly what you are doing,
   then it makes perfect sense to ask this one next.
It might seem ridiculous, but I can assure you the majority of
individuals and organizations know in their minds
what they really should be doing,
     and it's not what they are doing.
     Usually I hear responses like,
   "I know I really should be focusing on this or that, but I
spend so much time putting out fires, or going to meetings,
or whatever . . . I just can't seem to get around to it." Sound familiar?
For radical improvement to occur,
you must be doing what you know you should be doing.

Number 3.
What should you be doing NEXT?
Here's another simple step, what comes next? The great thing about even dynamic and dramatic results is that most of the steps you must take are simple ones. They're really easy to do, but as we've already mentioned, they're easier not to do. So the common practice is to choose easier, right?

Let what you should do next
BE what you actually do next.

The next step in the process is . . .
Ask. Then answer . . . It's a great action step.

And lastly, Number 4.
What should you NOT be doing?
This one can help clear the decks.
Identifying unproductive time and efforts being spent on things that in the big picture don't really matter. Can you think of one of these?
Something that you, or maybe a company or organization, got caught up in doing daily or weekly, spending valuable time and resources on that you really shouldn't be doing?

Like playing politics? Or protecting your turf? Or covering your . . .
You get the idea.
To really accomplish, to be productive, to achieve, to win, these 4 questions must be answered on a regular, continuing basis.

It's easy to do, but it's not common with the majority of individuals and organizations in today's marketplace.

"He who is firm in will
molds the world to himself."
—Johann Wolfgang von Goethe

THE UNCOMMON ART OF CHICK-FIL-A

A couple of years ago I delivered a luncheon keynote to an
area group of business leaders. We were discussing
uncommon companies, and I mentioned Chick-fil-A.

I made the statement that day that I feel
Chick-fil-A is ahead of 90% of the companies in
the marketplace because of HOW they do it!
That's a bold statement, but I believe it to be the truth.

Especially since I've had the chance to observe one Chick-fil-A
franchise in particular, firsthand for years. The Chick-fil-A
Arboretum in Charlotte. I've eaten there countless times as
a customer, but that's not my only reason. My daughter
has worked there for over two years, and if I had to offer evidence
to support my bold claim, Lindsay would be Exhibit A.

When she first started she was still in high school. She came home
with a "playbook" of sorts. A work book or a company manual,
Chick-fil-A calls it a GAME BOOK. It's pretty basic,
just paper and staples, but those 15 or so pages and the way they
drive the business make Chick-fil-A most certainly uncommon.

"Welcome," it says on the first page, with the now famous cow
holding the "EAT MOR CHIKIN" sign.
"I'm glad you're here with us, whether for a part-time
job or a career. I want you to enjoy working here."
Wow.
Then it goes on: What's in it for you . . .
Flexible hours, Sundays off, Experience in teamwork and
working with others, The opportunity to advance.

The History of Chick-fil-A, *(Do your employees know your history?)*
Their vision and standards and their focus and HOW WE DO IT.
It's all in there. And on the last page . . .

"We know you have the ability to excel!

We know you can do the job! So let's go!"
And then the team member, and their parents, sign it.
   Pretty impressive stuff.

Oh, I know it's a corporate chain, but you can only own a single
store in this chain. Only one. Make it your best one.
   And Art does just that.
I've known Art for many years and really admire the uncommon
way he captains his ship.
At any given time, he is responsible for coordinating the efforts of
   around 80 or so full- and part-time employees.
   Working them around school, soccer, class trips, and
important events and still providing top-shelf products
   and uncommon service from his team.

You don't have to take my word for it; the long lines daily speak
for themselves. And Art's Chick-fil-A is consistently among
   the top franchise stores in the country.

My daughter Lindsay absolutely loves working there. She loves
the people and the fun and the experience. For two years she had
several chances to leave there and make more money (20 or 30% more),
   but she didn't want to go. And that is also uncommon.

Eventually she did move on to another job as a server/hostess for
   a restaurant, but kept a shift or two regularly at Chick-fil-A
   just to hold on to that fun-and-friends part of her life there.

Moving to another job certainly made an impression on her about
   how truly uncommon things are at Chick-fil-A, which I
try to explain *(to her and others)* is exactly what makes them different
   from those other 90% of common companies
   still trying to figure it out.

One day I asked Lindsay to tell me why she thought
   Chick-fil-A and Art were different.
Why were they better in so many areas where other companies fail?

We talked a little about it and I challenged her, as a student
(now in college) to write me a "report" of sorts, just a few paragraphs . . .
she wrote 4 pages.

    So here, in her own words, is my 19-year-old daughter's
assessment of uncommon . . .

I began working at Chick-fil-A when I was 16 years old.
I have been there for almost three years, but what I have learned from
my experiences will stay with me for the rest of my life.
There are many reasons why Chick-fil-A is so uncommon,
the main one is Art.

Art is the owner of Chick-fil-A and an amazing guy.
Not that Chick-fil-A is struggling, [just the opposite] *and not that the*
employees there don't love it, [they do] *but just to become better*
and to know more about his business and the people who work in his
business, Art decided to take two months and dedicate these two
months for strictly getting to know his employees.

He would sit down every day for two hours and talk with each
employee. It took him several weeks to do this. When I first heard
about him doing this I thought, how could I possibly talk to him
about Chick-fil-A for two hours?
But the meeting was so much more than about Chick-fil-A.

Art would ask me things that were going on in my life, things that
were important to me, my "top-five priority list" in my life. He would
ask me my personal goals for the next year and my business goals for
the next year. It wasn't just about him and his company becoming
better, it was about him helping me to become better.

Art is always doing things like that. Every once in a while Art will
surprise the store with a reward for good sales that month.
Sometimes he'll give us gift certificates for the mall or take us
bowling and out for dinner or take all of us racing on an indoor track,
just to let us know that he appreciates us.

For my graduating class, Art took us white-water rafting . . .
that was uncommon— [good girl] *how many kids my age could say*
that their boss took them white-water rafting as a graduation gift?

Once a year the Chick-fil-A store takes a trip to Charleston, S.C.
It's not a trip to go sight-seeing and shopping,
it is a trip to lend a helping hand in the community.

We work with a ministry called Charleston Outreach;
one of the many things Charleston Outreach does is to tear down old
and rotting houses and rebuild them for free to then give them back
to the owners.

We would wake up in the mornings and head for the construction site.
Some days it would be tearing down a house, sometimes it would be
painting one. Sometimes it would be just sweeping and cleaning up
around a house. Then in the evening we'd go to a multi-housing site
to play with little children for a few hours.

It would soon get to where they would be waiting for us when we
arrived, and stare and wave at our bus as we left. These trips give us
time to really get to know each other as co-workers and as people.

There are new employees, old employees, managers, and even the
owner there, all in one place, becoming so much more than just
people who work together. We became people who cried together,
who laughed together, who played together. We became friends.

Chick-fil-A is so different because they have high standards that will
not be lowered for anything or anyone, or any amount of money. From
the owner down to the employees there is a mutual respect for one
another. The employees work hard for the company, and in return the
company takes good care of their employees.

I cannot remember one time when I have needed something, whether
it be a few dollars, a night off, a ride somewhere . . . I remember one
time my friend Erin and I were at Chick-fil-A after school [Erin also
works at Chick-fil-A], *we had gotten a ride there but did not have one*
to get back to the school for cheerleading practice.

We were stuck.

We felt comfortable enough to ask our manager for a ride. He told us that he couldn't leave the store then but handed us the keys to his truck. We said, are you sure? He told us just to be careful and come back to the store as soon as practice was over.

We were two 17-year-old girls who needed a ride to cheerleading practice [5 minutes away] *and our boss let us take his truck. The managers at Chick-fil-A always look out for us and have our best interests at heart. They are always so understanding, and if we need something that is in their power to get to us, they will!*

So what have I learned from Chick-fil-A?
More than I can put into words.

I've learned that no matter what is popular you have to do what you know is right. I've learned that you can never be too familiar with your work place. (i.e., know everything) *On the surface, I know everything there is to know about Chick-fil-A, how to work the register, how to cook the chicken, how to make the salads, how to mix the coleslaw . . .*

But underneath the surface there is so much more to be learned. Chick-fil-A has taught me that you can never know it all, you can always learn something more. Art has been the owner for over seven years, and every day he is learning how he can become better at his job, better than he was five years ago, better than he was one year ago, better today than yesterday (right Dad?).

Chick-Fil-A has taught me life principles that will stay with me forever.

Lindsay York

Wow. That's my girl!
Her own words on why Chick-fil-A is uncommon.
Thanks Lindsay.
And thanks Art.

Hail to the Chiefs . . .

The real Captains of American enterprise—
The Small Business Owner!

We call it Fast Business!
'Cause if you've ever started your own business,
  it can't happen fast enough.

And trust me, it's anything but small!

It's big risk, long hours, short funds, bills due,
    and making it happen . . . TODAY!   It's sudden-death overtime.
It's offense and defense and special teams all rolled into one.
    And you're it.
Make it happen . . . NOW.
GODSPEED!

> *"A man to carry on a successful*
> *business must have imagination.*
> *He must see things as in a vision,*
>   *a dream of the whole thing."*
> —Charles M. Schwab

Starting your own business sounds glamorous, doesn't it?
An adventure.

Exciting . . .

Courageous and Bold!
Great American Dream kinda stuff.
The Star Spangled Banner playing somewhere in the distance . . .
can you hear it?

Slight problem though,
New Biz Startup is NOT PRETTY.
Oh, it sounds pretty.

But it's the small business version of SURVIVOR.
Reward and immunity challenge. Somebody's getting voted out of
    the marketplace . . . soon. Impending customer tribal council.

Small business or just business in general.
    It's brutal.
It's brawling in the streets and wrestling alligators
    and questioning everything, every day.

It's trying to work *on* your business
    while you're busy working *in* your business.

When you decide to start your own business,
    look for human resources . . . friends, confidants, supporters,
encouragers, and anyone else you can remotely identify
    as a resource.

"One thing stirs me when I look back
    at my youthful days,
the fact that so many people gave me something
    or were something to me without knowing it."
—Albert Schweitzer

My Secret Weapon

I've had many friends and resources assist me
in getting my business to where it is today,
but none could be any more valuable than *MGC.*
It's sort of his code name, since 007 was already taken.

Michael is an amazing young man, wise beyond his years,
a model student, as well as a dynamic teacher.
He is an eager blur of activity with cell phone, laptop,
and various other personal electronic devices in tow,
and I can't imagine doing what I do today without him.

I've often told him that, and mean it every time I say it.
But then, he is a "launch pad" kind of guy.
He has been a true resource of mine, personally and professionally.
We have shared countless business meetings drawing on napkins
or crunching numbers in our respective living rooms.
Or laughing at our outrageous ideas during a round of golf.

He's heard most everything I have to say from the platform
but seems to respond like he's hearing it for the first time.

He is board member, radical thinker, millionaire mind, golf partner,
and friend. His is a depth that can only be appreciated by really
knowing him and what he stands for,
As well as his true willingness to help others.
My wish for you is that you find an MGC
when you begin building your business.

Thanks Michael.

When you start your own business you will learn
one of the truly dynamic principles of uncommon.
That there are times when incremental growth just isn't enough.
In fact, incrementalism is the greatest enemy of

Radical Growth!

What does that mean? Simple.

There are times when a 5%, 10%, or even a 20% increase

isn't enough.

When you start a new business at zero revenues,
a 20% increase is disaster. OB

(for those of you who've never been in that situation this means OUT of business).
What you've got to have in that case is a 1000% increase!

Radical, dynamic improvement.

When a woman becomes a mother for the first time,
she can't always depend on being a little better tomorrow
and slowly improving the next day . . . BOOM!
*There is swift and screaming persuasion for
her to be dramatically better in achieving the
desired results.*

Better go to work on some radical improvement in the
motherhood department and fast. The very nature
of becoming a parent demands it.

Sometimes it's not enough just to show "improvement."
Set your course for DYNAMIC IMPROVEMENT.

Most individuals don't understand that this kind of improvement
really is available!
It seems though, you seldom find it without a driving need to do so.

*"Men are not prisoners of fate,
but prisoners of their own minds."*

—Franklin Delano Roosevelt

Go For It

I once had the opportunity to share the speaking platform with
  ex-NFL quarterback Ken Stabler at a convention in Texas.
Ken is an "old-school" kind of guy with loads of great stories
  from his days with the Raiders and being coached by
  John Madden. Once after a game as Ken was getting dressed,
a reporter read to him the following quote from Jack London . . .

"I'd rather be ashes than dust.
I would rather my spark burn out in a brilliant blaze than be
stifled by dry rot. I would rather be a superb meteor,
  every atom a magnificent glow . . .
than be a sleepy, crumbling planet. For the proper function for
man is living, and not just existing.
  I shall not waste my days by trying to prolong them."

When Stabler was asked what that meant to him,
  he looked up and without hesitation responded . . .

"Throw Deep!"

Well said, Kenny. That pretty much sums it up.
Let's go down the field. Full speed ahead.
  That's the kind of guy Stabler is, *"no fear."*

Reckless, some might say, but his quarterbacking success says
otherwise. Fearless might be a better description, but at the
  very least you knew you had a guy who was in the fight
  with you to the end. Committed to your cause.
What if you had that same "go deep" mentality?
How would you answer this one . . .

"If you had no fear of failure . . . you would _____."

Think about that one for a moment.

If you had no fear that you might fail,
what would you do? What could you do?
You may be thinking to yourself . . .
"Michael, that's ridiculous. If I try something new, or
   something big, or most anything at all, sooner or later I'll fail."
True. But that's not the question.

The question is about having "no fear" of failure.
   It's knowing that some failure is required for
      dynamic achievement and radical growth.

But it's not fearing when you will fail.
   If you had no fear of failure, you'd fail more.
More often.
You'd dare, you'd attempt, you'd try new and bigger things
in your life and in your work. Wow.

I'm sure you can think of some individual right now that you view
as "having no fear" or having no fear of failure. It doesn't mean
      that this individual has never failed or will never fail. It means
      that they seem to have this fearless presence about them that
allows them to boldly go where some individuals have never
      gone before . . . dynamic results, in business or in life.

And chances are that individual you're thinking about is most
likely a top performer or high achiever. That sounds like a clue
      to success. Not being against failure, but knowing that some
failures are inevitable and pressing on with courage and conviction.

How would you ever learn to walk without falling first?
Or become an accomplished bike rider without a few spills,
   scraped knees *(five stiches in mine in fifth grade)* or skinned elbows.

Hey that gravel and pavement is painful, but it's nothing compared
   to the thrill of victory in learning to ride a bike!
      Going from not being able to ride, to riding is radical!

How Radical is Radical?
(a 10,000% increase)

OK, so it's not a 10 or 20 or 50 percent increase.
For you and your situation, it may not even be double or triple
    or 10 times what you do now.
        Radical for you could mean as much as 100 or
1,000 times better or greater than the results you now get.

Becoming 10% better wasn't going to help
NASA get to the moon or
        Chrysler turn things around or
            Walt Disney create the Magic Kingdom, or
                Fed Ex get it there overnight.

There had to be breakthrough results.
    Like nothing they'd ever done before. That's radical.

Try it.
Aim high, and see where you can go.
Try some radical, dynamic, breakthrough ideas and
    see where it takes you.
There are loads of examples of radical improvement.
Here's one you may not have considered . . .
Parking.
Or more specifically, parking meters and their role in radical,
revenue-generating improvement!

Think about this.
When you park your car downtown in almost any city it's a quarter
        for 10 minutes or 30 minutes or whatever.
    Let's use my city, Charlotte, North Carolina.

I can park for 30 minutes by putting a quarter in the meter.
But on the 31st or 32nd minute, if one of Charlotte's finest checks
    that meter and it's empty, what does it cost me now?
Another quarter?
Maybe two?

Try twenty-five dollars.
TWENTY-FIVE DOLLARS?

That's the price for a parking ticket in downtown Charlotte,
    for a minute or few minutes of miscalculation on my part
(or calculated risk), the city receives a RADICAL revenue
improvement of 10,000%!
(Park by a hydrant and it goes to $100 . . . even more radical.)

Get the idea?
How can you create radical breakthrough improvement for you
    or your business or your company?
Is it possible?
You bet. It's already been done.

WHO'S YOUR COMPETITION?
Think about this.
Your competition is EVERYBODY!

I've spent many years in the advertising and marketing arena.
Working with and for hundreds of clients in radio, TV, newspaper,
    and magazines. I'm seldom surprised when I ask a prospect
        or even a customer,
"Who do you feel is your competition?"

Inevitably they'll say another widget company or a company that
is "like them." If they're a bank, then they say the competition is
    some other financial entity. Not long ago, many people might
have given a "dot-com" answer to the competition question.

But even that's changed or changing today.
My answer to them is "Mr. Biz, I'd like you to consider for a moment that **everyone in the entire civilized world is competing with you** and your business!"

Wow, that's a bold statement or a really odd one.
It's probably not one he's heard before. It's atypical.
But it's true.

There are bazillions of messages bombarding you every day through every media outlet and in new areas every day. Thousands of voices yelling and screaming and pleading, *"Hey, look at us."*

They're all competing for my attention, and your attention as consumers.

So when I say that EVERYONE is the competition, I mean they all compete to get you and I to focus on their message for the longest possible time. Some of these messages I won't hear at all. I'll be in the bathroom, or making a sandwich, or reading,
Or driving, listening to tapes, probably of me
(kidding, probably Zig or Mr. Rohn).
Or I may be there when the commercial voices cry out to me, but I'm not in the market or not paying attention. Whatever I'm doing, I'm tuning out, not receiving or responding to their message.

What's that sound . . .

This is what's called the *"White Noise Theory."*
After a while it all blends together into oblivion.
Sort of like leaving your window open so you can hear the ocean or keeping the fan on at night.
After a while you become accustomed to these sounds to the point of not even consciously hearing them.

They're just white noise. You'd miss them if they weren't there, but you can't remember them not being there.
You've grown to the point of tuning them out.

So, what's the answer for Mr. Biz?

Well, you can't have no advertising or marketing.
    Then you're not even in the mix;
you're not even invited to the white noise party.

You have to spend a certain amount *(of time and money)* just
    to be there, but then there has to be something over and above
to *create IMPACT!*

So you can jump out of the background noise and lock on for
    a minute or few seconds. Something that sets you apart.
        In the advertising business, it's called branding
or brand awareness. Making consumers aware that
    you're good, that they can be comfortable with your name,
        your brand, your store, and your products or services.

But for most companies, especially those trying to reach the
boomers and "fifty-somethings," let's say age 29–59, upscale,
    active lifestyles, home, kids, soccer practice, and a wish list . . .
        there's nothing, I mean NOTHING, you have that's going
    to interrupt their busy boomer hectic lifestyle and have them
drop everything they're doing and rush to the phone
        or drive right over to take advantage of your
        annual once-in-a-lifetime-we-should-be-going-
            out-of-business-red-tag-or-half-off-blow-out-sale!

Come on. This marketplace is more sophisticated than ever before.
They've seen it all, tried most of it, and sent half of it back.

You have to be better than that to get their business.

They've got to be comfortable with your brand, and when they move
through the steps of that purchase from the *initial awareness*
        to *in-the-market-for,* to <u>*about-to-buy,*</u>
you want to be on their short list. Maybe the only one on the list.

The key is being consistent
    and being UNCOMMON with your message.

Now, having said that, there's a time to be patient,
and a time to be RADICAL, over-the-top.
Think about this . . .
If all of a sudden you had a company van
(you know one of those panel wagons or delivery type van) . . .

What Message Would You Put On The Side Of Your Van?

The name of your biz?
That's uncommon, huh?

If you had say a sheet-metal business and your name was Joe . . .
hmmm, let's see . . . I know, how about Joe's Sheet Metal!
Wow, how'd we ever come up with that one?
Uncommon says we've got to do better than common.
Think about what sets you apart from everyone else.
Get it down to the most basic form, and decide what
message you want to send to the world.

I have a friend whose business is a coffee service.

Dean is a long-time friend and a second-generation driver for
his own coffee company. We've had lots of discussions on sports
and business and how we can solve many of the problems of
the president, the pope, and our friends.
And on occasion we talk about marketing our own businesses.

One day I called him up and said,
"Hey, I've got your new marketing campaign . . ."
What made me think about this was seeing a coffee truck
for a company, let's call it Blank & Blank Coffee,
and of course on the side of the truck in huge letters was . . .

Blank & Blank Coffee
Fine coffees, teas, and juices.

Hmmmm. That must be a powerful marketing message.
A radical branding statement.
Otherwise why would so many companies do it?
They put their name in huge letters, but they don't tell me why
I should pick them over all the other companies who are like them,
or who I think are like them.

Dean has a fleet of new vans with his drivers carrying his coffees
all over Little Rock, Arkansas. But putting **Dean's Coffee**
on the side of those vans stops short of any kind of memorable
marketing message that has an impact. So we added these words . . .

"We make it easy to enjoy a great cup of coffee."

Bang.
We didn't say it was the best
(although I've had lots of his coffee and it really is a good cup of coffee),
but he's going to make it easy for YOU!

Isn't that what you want when you get to the office? Easy?
A good cup of coffee without having to dig around for coffee filters
or sugar or running down to the store because
you've run out of coffee?
What sets you apart from all the other stale and mundane
messages everyone's hurling at
your prospective customers?

So the next time you think about your competition,
*think about YOU, little ol' you,
mixing it up with the rest of the world.*

Because especially today, that's the battle.
You vs. R.O.W., "rest of world."
They're all out there with a "ME.com," and they're gunning for you!

I'll share just one other story in this area.

I was making my way back to my room one night after speaking at
Moody Gardens Hotel in Galveston Island, Texas.
It is an incredible property with a great story,
but this story is about one of the merchants
on property.

Casa Blanca.

It's a boutique in the hotel.
As I'm walking by at around 10:30 that night, the sign in the
window caught my eye. It read . . .

"In the event of *a gift or fashion emergency,* call us anytime day or night."

And then the phone number.

I was struck by the message.
It was uncommon.
Not call us when we open, or except on weekends,
It said to call ANYTIME day or night.
The next day I saw a gentleman in the store and
stopped in to ask about the message.
"Do you ever get calls in the middle of the night?"
Oh yes, absolutely, he says.
We talked for a while, and I was most impressed.

Now here's the thing.
You don't call up at 3 a.m. just to look around.
No, it's a gift or fashion emergency!
And bring your checkbook. You're a buyer!

Casa Blanca has provided uncommon service
    to hundreds of hotel guests who return to their homes
in Charlotte or Chicago or London and continue buying from
    this unique boutique as long-distance and lasting customers.
Cool!

Ritchard and Susan, the owners of Casa Blanca,
    have sent the message to you and me, the customer,
that they're "uncommon," and we noticed . . . certainly I did.

Just on my way back to my hotel room late one night, and bang!
And now here I am, years later, not just remembering but telling you
    and lots of others about their uncommon attitude
    on serving the marketplace.
Want to know more about Casa Blanca?
    That gift or fashion emergency number is 409-765-7724.
        Be sure to tell them Michael says hello.

What's your message?
Get prepared, or get waxed.
    How are you and your business delivering the
            message that you're uncommon?
My daily reminder of this one is a small poster on my wall
    that shows two eyes coming out of a dark background,
eyes that obviously belong to a tiger. And the caption reads simply,
"Lead . . . or be lunch!" Good luck, Mr. Phelps.

> *"Make no little plans,*
>   *for they have no magic to*
>   *stir man's blood."*
>   —Daniel Burnham

The LIST of Uncommon

→

A quick read.
Spaced repetition.
Remember spaced repetition?
It's how you learned your multiplication tables.
So let's use it now to learn about becoming uncommon.

Here's a quick look at some of the
principles of uncommon, sprinkled with just a bit of
"inexpensive" advice . . . for the workplace and for life.

Working Wisdom
Or just a few notes from my journals
on living life . . .

The little things that make a big difference often go unnoticed in
"common" organizations.
Remember, your goal is to become UNCOMMON!

So here goes . . .

Long hours aren't the best measure of performance or results. What are you actually accomplishing in the time you're "working?"

Understand the difference between spending time and investing time. One means it is gone forever, the other means it will continue to return rewards and results.

Time management is a poor objective and
"mis" communication.

Time cannot be managed;
>it is oblivious to you and me, and our feeble
attempts to harness it.

"Me" management is a better objective.

The next time you hear someone say,

"I don't have the time,"
>look him in the eye and tell him
>how special he really is.

>"You're getting the maximum
>amount of time the law allows!"
24/7, that's all there is as far as we know,
>and we're all getting it.

The question is

>what will you do with it for the

greatest return on results

>for your life?

Don't be so serious.
Loosen up; life is short,
   and there are enough stiffs and bores.
Laugh a little and take time for fun.

A survey of top performers showed
   they spent 8-10 hours for recreation every week . . .
or at least they said they did.

   "Re-Create" your enjoyment for living every day.
People will absolutely notice.

Simplify. Make your life and work easier,
and the lives and work of those around you.

Don't bring problems to your supervisors
without possible solutions or ideas
   to improve them.
      They get that enough from everyone else,
         be uncommon . . . people will notice.

Don't feed gossip at all.
Refuse to nurture poison, and it will cease to grow and
spread. It's the law of sowing and reaping.

Help the process along,
    give your boss your own *"review"* of your
performance. Be Honest and look for the areas where
you can improve,
    then tell what and how you'll do it.

*Be always in the process of
becoming.*

*Work on improving all areas of
communication* and your skill in getting
    your point across clearly with persuasion and
    understanding. *It'll serve you well in life
    as well as business.*

Don't use profanity. Ever.
You don't need it. You may not see people cringe
    when you use it, but many will, and they will
always remember. Even if you slip once in a
    while, keep it as your goal.

Take responsibility and share credit.
This makes you uncommon,
    since most will take credit and
    give away blame.

Time is NOT money.
You can make more money,
    but once time is lost it can never be regained.

No matter how much you want to go back and change
something you regret, it is not for sale and cannot be
bought at any price . . . **time is so much more
than money.**

Make friends everywhere,
    every day. This will speak highly of you . . .
and so will they.

Be confident and courageous.
It's uncommon. If you're not, go to work on the
    process of "becoming."

Keep a journal. It's not just a diary,
   but a place to keep your notes on life and business.
Keep it in a bound book, where you'll always
   know how to find what happened in a meeting or how
   you felt about something while others will forget or
   misplace these important items.
It's uncommon.

Don't neglect celebration.
       It is the candle on the cake of expectation and
accomplishment. Any behavior you want to see repeated
must be acknowledged and celebrated so others will
want to go there again.

*Develop a mind-set that confirms to
others that you are a champion.*
Not arrogance or condescension, but a positive,
can-do attitude that is contagious.

If someone says to you,
"I wish I could be more like you,"
       you'll know you're getting there.

Everything is YOUR job.
Never say that common phrase that makes you a
"non-resource" who can't affect how a
situation works out.
Find a way to make it happen.
People absolutely will notice.

Treat your job like it's your own business. Become the CEO of "YOU, Inc."

Work harder on you than you do on your job. When you get better, it will affect the results you get on any job you do.

Take a vacation.
Don't be a martyr for the company.
You'll get better results, at home and at work, when you take the time to recharge your battery and get a fresh mind-set.

Never sell your vacation time or let it expire;
it's worth more than money ... it's your life.

Whether you get training or not,
become a continuous learner.

Always be in the process of
learning something *that improves*
your skills and makes you better.

Get excited. *About something!*
Excitement is an emotion that fires your fuel
and something you need to feel once in a while.

Make time for life, not just work.
Some clichés are true, like the one about "all work and
no play" making you dull.
Life, and work, are much better when your
tools are SHARP!

If you find yourself always answering the question,
"How are you?" by saying,
"I'm stressed," *change something,*
so you can have a better answer tomorrow.

Experience isn't everything.

It's good to a point, but change demands you be better today than you were 5 or 10 years ago.

New procedures, tools, and techniques are no better than the old ways if you don't use them.

Don't be driving a covered wagon while people are passing you in planes.
Wake up and get better.

Take your experience and invest it into today to get dramatic results, because you can.

People will notice.

Be open to new ideas. Remember, history proves that the crowd is seldom on-board at the beginning of a new way of doing something.

Be willing to make
daring mistakes.
Make them faster than anyone else,
make corrections and adjustments and then
make better mistakes.

Something your spouse and kids
will never tell you . . .
"I'm sure glad you put in all that
extra time at the office." Or "Sure
wish we didn't have to do all these
family things together."

Give value to all the parts of your life,
including your family. Call it balance or whatever
you like *but don't miss this part of the*
life treasure.
Once it passes you by, there's no getting it back.
And regrets or "I'm sorry" or "I wish"
is a poor memory to be left with.

There is a time to listen to good music. But don't overdo it. Make time for good messages like cassettes, books on tapes, *or something that contributes to your learning.* Driving in your car can be the best "higher education" you ever get if you spend it as quality listening time.

Embrace new technology. Learning, not just training, will make your life easier and better.

Become known as the leader of a "construction" crew, not a demolition driver or a one-man wrecking ball. Anyone can tear things down, but a *master builder is uncommon.*

Be above playing politics. Don't lie, pander, pout, put down, or try to have the biggest something by making everyone else's look small.

It's temporary positioning and does irreparable harm to your reputation among customers and co-workers.

Know the real definition of CUSTOMER.

It's not just someone who can buy your product or service. You have customers all around you.

Think about this uncommon definition . . .
The Object of Your Communication!

Your spouse, child, co-worker, manager, they all have a need to "buy you."

Take care of all the customers around you, and you'll find you're attracting more loyal customers who think you are the best.

The customer isn't always right,
   but they are always the customer.

And you have the power to make all of your customers feel special.

The perception of salespeople?

How about

obnoxious, pushy, say anything,
do anything, less than truthful . . .

Why is that?

Poor management and poor techniques

have caused this terrible impression of the most valuable asset most organizations possess, **the individuals entrusted with generating the revenues that pay everyone's salaries.** It's up to you and me to change the perception and change the outcome.

Understand that whatever job you do is a part of the process that provides a product or service that **someone has to sell and someone has to buy. Otherwise, you're out of a job.** Try to gain a new empathy for the salespeople who drive the revenues for your company. They're not all out to make your life miserable.

Use personal communication.

Handwritten notes and even email and voice mail
messages that acknowledge a job well done
     or encourage someone to hang in there.

It's easy to do, but easier NOT to do.

Most choose easier, but you can be uncommon just by
choosing . . . easy. If it's easy to do,
     why not give it a try. People will notice.

MVPs are everywhere.

Be a most valuable player,

an impact player.

Be known for your skills and attitude and contribution.
People should be asking
"How could we ever make it without _____?"
Become more valuable.

Take time to THINK. **Really think.**

Quiet time, creative time where you can be struck by
the lightning of an idea. Expose yourself to creative
time and places. Don't ask how . . . **if you search,
you will find.** It is an ancient wisdom that has been
proven over and over.

All companies have managers,

not all have leaders. And most don't have enough leaders. Managers are needed to count and control and inventory, but

someone has to share a vision,

a cause that can inspire an organization or group of individuals to achieve something incredible or go somewhere they've never been before.

A leader propels an organization in the direction of dynamic achievement.

Find and develop more leaders.

Leaders are wherever you find them. They may be anywhere in an organization. Some receptionists will make great leaders.

And some managers couldn't make it as a receptionist. Don't say "**If I were a VP, I'd make some changes around here!**"

Start right where you are and make changes that show your leadership qualities and abilities.

Someone just might notice.

Don't try to impress with "things."
People are impressive, not things.

Use the law of inertia to your advantage.
That means "DO SOMETHING!"
Get your body in motion and it will tend to remain in motion, taking you in the direction of completing any task no matter how difficult. Just begin, and "the law" works for you.

Trust is a huge matter and a
quality that takes great measures of time to build but only a moment to destroy.

Be Trust Worthy . . .
worthy of the trust of others.

Treat all work as a "project," meaning
it has a beginning and an ending. You should know when you are finished so that you can
celebrate and then begin a new project.

Don't worry about being "interesting,"
be *INTERESTED* in others and you
will be seen as one of the most interesting
people they know. It's uncommon.

Ever notice how the people around you who have
"*nothing to do*" always seem to want to do it with
you? You will be known by the company you keep.
Be uncommon by association.

Be Gracious. It becomes you.

Don't get caught up in your own "kingdom" and think all
the subjects are loyal and understand a
mission statement that sounds like this . . .
"We strive to blah, blah, blah . . . and serve our customer
and blah, blah, blah . . ." What does that mean? It's
communication, but nobody understands it. Have a
clear objective that makes everyone in the
organization say, "I got it."

Communication doesn't prevent miscommunication; in fact, in many cases it causes it or contributes to it. Strive for understanding. By its very definition, understanding prevents misunderstanding.

Keep it simple.

One of the greatest mission statements ever ...

"To deliver the package the very next day ... regardless!"

—Federal Express

Try your own personal mission statement that says "I will (do whatever you choose) no matter what!" then sign it.

Do something impossible.
The impossible is done every day ...

Light, Flight, The 4-minute mile, all were said to be impossible once upon a time. What radical dynamic improvement are you working on?

Work on solutions to problems.
 Improvements to root causes,
not symptoms.

If morale is poor it's not a morale problem,
    it's a result of some other root cause that is
producing poor morale. Find out, and attack the real
problem.

Be personable, and PERSONAL.
    Never deliver good news or bad news any way but
    in person. It shows
respect for the other person
and earns respect for you.

Life is short. Love what you do.
If you don't love what you do, do something else;
    or at least begin planning for the day when you can
    do something you will love to do.
        The common thing to do is just complain.
Be uncommon.

Whipping animals will not be tolerated in our society, but organizations still consider it acceptable to berate and verbally abuse their workers. Be above emotional whipping to get the results you want.

Encourage, instruct, and inspire; it's uncommon, and one of the true clues of successful companies and organizations.
Try it.

Read a book. Almost any book to start. Once you begin reading, it leads to reading more. *Create a library* that allows you to develop not just knowledge but a love for learning. A great man once remarked that
     even though he'd not read every book in his library
... (yet), just standing in the presence of all those books made him feel smarter. It also eventually instilled a desire to read as many of them as he could. *Try it, it's easy.*
     It's just a few less TV reruns.
     (Watch less TV; it's uncommon)

Make lists.

Lists are powerful tools. Check off the things you accomplish and notice how it makes you feel. List the 3 or 4 <u>MOST IMPORTANT</u> things you'll do today, everyday, and see what you actually accomplish in less time.

How often does "Change" happen?

Right now. Make sure it happens "in you" as often as it's happening around you.

Embrace change, keep up the learning curve.

Go to work everyday like it's the day of your annual performance review . . .

it is.

Don't smoke. It kills.
Not maybe . . . it's a proven fact!
If you smoke anyway, don't do it in the front of
    the building with all the other smokers.
The only thing that smells worse
than the smoke is the stench of all the complaining and
gossip that goes on there daily.

Separate yourself, or become known by the
company you keep as a smoker, complainer, gossiper,
and common malcontent.
    Fair or not, it's true.

Why is it companies don't give
"NON-SMOKE" breaks 3 or 4 times
    a day to those workers who don't smoke.
Most smokers end up with an extra
lunch hour every day.
This can often cause dissent and
    morale problems among workers.
                        Pay Attention.

Treat everyone with respect.
    Not with respect for their job or position,
but respect for them as a person.

It will gain you much more respect than you can ever give away.

"Think Big! No one ever heard of Alexander The Average."

Make sure everyone knows the answer to these 2 questions . . .

1. What's my job?
2. How am I doing?

There you have it.

Just a few of the notes I've taken
in my attempt to keep up the learning curve
as a good student.

Capture your notes on life and business and reread them periodically
to see how you're doing. And to make sure that you're not making
the same mistakes over and over.
It's uncommon.

"It's supposed to be hard.
If it wasn't hard,
everyone would do it.
The hard is what makes it great!"
—Tom Hanks as Jimmy Dugan in
A League of Their Own

ENJOY THE RIDE

There are lots of great works of inspiration
and great words of wisdom. I've tried my best to give you at least
   a sampling of just a few of them in the pages of this book.

One of my favorite writings is called
"The Station," and I've included it here for you to enjoy.
It struck me when I first read it, but as I get older
      its meaning seems more and more poignant.

The Station

Tucked away in our subconscious is an idyllic vision.
We see ourselves on a long trip that spans the continent.
      We are traveling by train, and out the window we drink in
      the passing scene of cars on nearby highways.
      At children waving at a crossing, of cattle grazing on a
distant hillside, of row upon row of corn and wheat.

Flat lands and valleys, mountains and rolling hillsides.
City skylines and village homes. But uppermost in our mind is
      the final destination, on a certain day at a certain hour
      when we will pull into the station.

Bands will be playing, flags will be waving, once we get there
      so many wonderful dreams will come true and the pieces of
      our lives will fit together like a completed jigsaw puzzle.
Oh, how we pace the aisles, counting the minutes . . . waiting,
            waiting for the station.

When we reach the station, *"Oh, that will be it,"* we cry.
When I'm 18, when I buy a new car, when I put my
      last kid through college, when I have paid off the mortgage,
when I get a promotion, when I reach the age of retirement . . .
I shall live happily ever after.

Sooner or later we must all realize there is no station.
No place to arrive at once and for all.
For the true joy of life is in the trip;
   the station is only a dream that constantly outdistances us.

So stop pacing the aisles and counting the miles;
     Instead, climb more mountains, eat more ice cream,
  go barefoot more often, swim more rivers, watch more sunsets,
laugh more, cry less. Life must be lived as we go along.
The station will come soon enough.

Wow.
Just a few words written down one day by Robert Hastings,
maybe in a blank book, and captured here, for you to enjoy.
Preserved for life.

What's so important in your life that you absolutely must
write it down? So you and others can enjoy it whenever they
     might come across it and read it again or discover it
       for the very first time?

Try it. It's powerful.

"And now I have finished a work
   that neither the wrath of love, nor fire,
  nor the sword, nor devouring age
    shall be able to destroy."
         —Ovid

I've been an entrepreneur for most of my life,
but I've also spent many of those years working in a
corporate-executive, fast-paced, stress-packed environment.
   And during that time I've seen
        many high-powered top guns whose lives
outside their business were a wreck.

Oh, they had two or three homes and new cars
   and expensive suits and lots of "things,"
        but they got little enjoyment out of life.
And came to the realization much too late that they had
given little value to anyone outside of their 70-hour-a-week jobs.

I am fortunate and thankful that my life has had lots of flowers,
lots of bird feeders, lots of porch swings, and hand-holding, and
   good-night kisses, and quality time with loved ones,
      lots of questions, and lots of answers.
   And even still small voices when everything was midnight-quiet.

The journey has been so much more
        than any singular destination could ever be.
   And the great part is, I've already learned how to enjoy it.
      Even better, it's not over yet.

"This is Life like no other . . .
   This is The Great Adventure!"
      —Steven Curtis Chapman, *The Great Adventure*

I hope you enjoy this book for what it's intended to be.
How we can all get on with becoming better at whatever it is
   we want to be better at.
   Don't waste any more time standing still
      or stuck in pause.
Get on the way!

The journey is life, and it's fantastic!

And the One who created you
has also created so much fullness for you to enjoy.

I want to challenge you to do more!
Climb more mountains.
See more sunsets.
Take more walks along the beach.
Read more.
Listen more.
Study more.
Pray more.
Laugh more and love more!

I can't wait to hear about your experiences when I see you.
And I will see many of you.

That's a goal of mine, and here I have gone and written it down,
so you know what that means.

May God Richly Bless You!
The Best Is Yet To Be!

Here's to your uncommon success,

Michael

"Somehow I can't believe that there are
any heights that can't be scaled
by a man who knows
the secrets of making dreams
come true.
This special secret —
curiosity, confidence,
courage,
and constancy;
and the greatest of all
is confidence.
When you believe in a thing,
believe in it all the way,
implicitly and unquestionably."

—Walt Disney

That man is a **success**
who has lived well,
laughed often, and loved much.
Who has gained the
respect of intelligent men
and the love of children.
Who has filled his niche
and accomplished his task.
Who leaves the world

a better place
than he found it,
whether by an
improved poppy,
a perfect poem,
or a rescued soul.
Who never lacked
appreciation for earth's beauty
or failed to express it.
Who always looked for the best in
others and *gave the best he had.*

I wish for you the very best that life has to offer and
may you be a success in every way!

Michael York

YOUR PERSONAL JOURNAL PAGES

My notes and what I learned from Michael's book . . .

Your Personal
Journal Pages

Your Personal
Journal Pages

YOUR PERSONAL JOURNAL PAGES

*YOUR PERSONAL
JOURNAL PAGES*

YOUR PERSONAL JOURNAL PAGES

Your Personal
Journal Pages

$\mathcal{M}$ichael York

The Michael York Company, Inc.
"Rock Solid Training"

4801 East Independence Blvd., Suite 1000
Charlotte, North Carolina 28212
For speaking or booking information, contact us at
704.622.2400 or email, leader@michaelyork.com
www.MichaelYork.com